The Working Man's Hand:

Celebrating Woody Guthrie
Poems of Protest and Resistance
2023

Paul Juhasz, Editor

FINE DOG
PRESS

Editor's Introduction

After more than a decade of collaboration with Woody Guthrie's daughter, Nora, who was curating a collection of her father's unreleased lyrics, the Boston Celtic band, The Dropkick Murphys released the album *This Machine Still Kills Fascists* in September 2022. Nora characterized the unpublished lyrics as words that "needed to be said—or screamed, and if you need lyrics screamed, you call the Dropkick Murphys." Because of this seemingly odd pairing (although The Dropkick Murphys 2006 hit, "I'm Shipping Out to Boston," was also a rendition of Woody Guthrie lyrics) we are invited to not only experience new, never-heard-before Guthrie songs, but also to be reminded of Woody Guthrie's essential voice of opposition to oppression and injustice.

Woody Guthrie, songwriter, poet and Oklahoma folk hero, was a champion of the disenfranchised, of minorities, of the working class, and an advocate for justice, using his music to speak out against injustice in all its forms. His love and understanding for the common man, for the blue-collar backbone of America, is a consistent theme throughout his canon. His newly released song, "The Last One'," is an acknowledgement of the exploitation and the hardships of that blue-collar experience. Guthrie writes:

> She's upside down, she's broke apart
> And getting worse every day;
> A workin' man's hand is the hardest card
> In the whole damn deck to play.

This exploitation continues today, as wealth and power become increasingly concentrated into the hands of the few, protected by a political and social apparatus designed to obfuscate, gaslight, and gerrymander. To this end, we are pleased to bring you this 2023 edition of our anthology, with the theme, "The Workin' Man's Hand."

- Paul Juhasz
March, 2023

Woody Guthrie Poetry Group: A History

By Dr. Dorothy Alexander

(updated 21 March 2022 by Jessica Isaacs)

The Woody Guthrie Poets of Oklahoma began in 2005 when twenty poets gathered to read their poetry at the annual Guthrie Folk Festival held each July in Woody's hometown of Okemah, Oklahoma. The group was chosen and assembled by Carol Hamilton, former Poet Laureate of Oklahoma, and George Wallace, poet and teacher of Long Island, New York, who presented the idea to the Guthrie Festival Directors in Okemah. David Amram has been an important member of the founding group and has provided musical accompaniment every year for the poets at the Okemah Woody Guthrie Festival readings.

The purpose and the goal of the Woody Guthrie Poetry Group is:

> To *memorialize in poetry the history and culture of working people and to perpetuate the ideals and goals of equality for the working class, and themes that Woody Guthrie espoused and promoted in his art.*

> To *raise world consciousness of the labor and political movements of the thirties through the fifties, and of the* present *time. To give commentary on the social and political environment in the 21ˢᵗ Century, as Woody Guthrie might see it.*

Each poet reads their original poems written to commemorate the themes Woody Guthrie espoused and promoted in his art and his work, along with depicting the era about which Woody wrote and sang.

The readings immediately attracted large audiences at the festival and were soon expanded to additional venues throughout the state. Other readings were soon added and the poets began pre-reading gatherings where they assembled printed collections of their poems for handouts at Okemah. After their first appearance at the festival, members of the group were invited to read and speak at poetry and art festivals, public library programs, civic events, writing workshops, genealogy societies and in many other gatherings in both rural and urban communities in Oklahoma as well as in surrounding states of Texas, Kansas and New Mexico.

The group members change from year to year but the original thread remains the same. Always sticking to the Woody Guthrie principles and applying them to current culture. The original group included (besides George Wallace and Carol Hamilton) Al Turner, Jeanetta Calhoun Mish, Nathan Brown, Carl Sennhenn, Dorothy Alexander, Francine Ringold, Larry Griffin, Richard Dixon, Richard Rouillard, and the late Jim Spurr, who read every year until his death in late 2014. The only person who has never missed a reading since the beginning is Dorothy Alexander. Carol Hamilton and George Wallace continued to organize and curate the readings through 2009. In 2010 Dorothy Alexander and Nathan Brown assumed the task of organizing and promoting the readings. By then the number of poets applying to read had become so numerous that Dorothy and Nathan added additional readings, along with poetry writing workshops, held prior to the Okemah reading, in order to give an opportunity for as many poets as possible to add to the legacy of Woody Guthrie. These venues included the Istvan Art Gallery in Oklahoma City, the Beans & Leaves Coffee House, the Paramount OKC Theatre, and members' private homes.

The number of readings dedicated to remembering Woody Guthrie and his legacy increased to four during Festival week, i.e. one at the Benedict Street Deli in Shawnee, on Thursday evening of Festival Week (July 13, 2017) which has a featured reader followed by an Open Mic; one on Friday night (July 14) with a slate of juried readers selected by the panel; one on Saturday morning (July 15) at the Methodist Church in Okemah; and one on Sunday afternoon (July 16) at the Woody Guthrie Center, Brady Art District in Tulsa. Both the OKC and the Tulsa readings feature a selection of poets chosen by Jessica and the panel.

In 2010 the first anthology of Woody poems was published by Village Books Press, edited by Dorothy Alexander, entitled *Travelin' Music*; and in 2012, the 100th anniversary of Woody's birth, saw publication of the second anthology entitled *Elegant Rage*, featuring the art of famed artist, Bert Seabourn, on its cover. Poets throughout the U.S. and from many foreign countries have published poetry in the anthologies.

A third anthology was published by Village Books Press in 2017, *Ain't Gonna Be Treated This Way*. edited by Dorothy Alexander and Terri Cummings, with cover art and design by Devey Napier. A fourth anthology *Speak Your Mind*, also published by Village Press Books and edited by Dorothy Alexander, followed in 2019.

In 2015, Jessica Isaacs, professor at Seminole State College, assumed the mantle of coordinator and curator of the Woody Guthrie Poets of Oklahoma, with a panel of associates consisting of Dorothy Alexander, Terri Cummings, Nathan Brown, Ben Myers and Branwyn Holroyd. Paul Juhasz assumed the role of coordinator and curator in 2019.

The Woody Poets are dedicated to assuring the continuation of the tradition which has had a momentous impact on the Oklahoma literary community and the legacy of Oklahoma's own Woody Guthrie.

A Tribute to Dr. Dorothy Alexander, Whose Spirit Endures

By Jessica Isaacs

When I was first asked to write this tribute, I thought, I don't know if I can do this. This is really, really hard. How could I ever do justice by Dorothy – Dorothy, whose life always seemed to me to be so much larger than life and whose spirit seemed boundless? I wrestled with the decision for days, and then in typical Dorothy fashion, she appeared one night in my dream, looked me straight in the eye, and said, "Yes, you can, Jess. Of course you can," and I knew then that I could do it. And that is who Dorothy is. Her spirit endures, living on in the lives of the people she loved and encouraged, and who loved her. Her brightly burning spirit of justice and truth and poetry endures.

When my Nanny, my grandmother, died, I wrote her obituary. Her name was also Dorothy. This tribute to another beloved Dorothy, my mentor and friend, is the second hardest thing I've ever been asked to write. There is no easy way through grief. And there is no right way to go about it, nor is there a "time stamp" for when it begins and ends. Grief ebbs and flows, like Dorothy's influence that lives on in each of us and the words we craft on our pages, the ways we love and support and encourage one another.

Dorothy was a woman of action, and she lives on in our actions. She made a place at the "poetry table" for so many of us, and she didn't hog the spotlight. She made a way in the darkness for us to follow. For that, I will be forever grateful and cherish the time I had to know her.

We love you and cherish you, Dr. Dorothy Alexander. This one's for you.

With greatest love and respect,
Jessica

The Judge
for Dorothy

waving her red hat, shooing
those Greedy Bastards
out of Oklahoma, out
of New Mexico, hell,
out of the whole damn west,
taking on the whole
state of the union,
suffering no fools,
but long-suffering though,
of those who deserve it,
long-loving and fast-sticking
to justice, to honor,
to the fragility of life,
judge and poet, balance and weight,
the lion-hearted, yellow-dogged,
red-hatted reconciler,
still holding out hope
for this red state

Order of Poets

The Working Man's Hand

Alan Berecka *is the author of five books of poetry, the latest* A Living is Not a Life: A Working Title *(2021, Black Spruce Press), which explores the concept of work, was a finalist in the Hoffer Awards. He earned his living for many years as librarian at Del Mar College in Corpus Christi. In January 2023, he finally lived long enough to put down the date due stamp and retire. He and his wife Alice reside in Sinton, Texas where they raised their two now-adult children.*

Blue-Collar Heaven

My father never got a paid day off—
no sick days, no holidays, not even
Christmas, so he worked on every Eve,
and birthday, dragged himself to work
with fevers, and stitches, often over
my mother's protests because, "The God-
damned bills won't pay themselves."

His tin knocker's union had a healthy
strike fund, so he never voted to ratify
a single contract, no matter how
reasonable the terms, no matter
if Jesus Christ himself returned to Utica
as a union boss and preached on the value
of ratification, my old man's mind
would have remain unchanged,
even if he knew his thumbs down
would place his back-pew Catholic soul
in peril, because nothing he could imagine
came closer to Eden than sitting
on a cheap lawn chair in his backyard
on a weekday afternoon while nursing
a cold brew and watching his grass grow
all the while knowing that a fat check
from the union sat in his bank account
answering his most basic of prayers.

1

Vocational Education

One year while home on my summer break,
as part of my town job, I was given a three foot
crowbar with a special tip and told to pry up
every manhole cover in Marcy, New York.
After I wrestled the forty-pound Frisbees
up and to the side of the hole, I peered
down and through the stench into the filth below
and observed the flow of sewer water,
watched turds, soiled paper and a few used Kotex
or spent condoms sail by with great relief, for my job
was to free any clogs that kept the waste from flowing
with the aid of gravity to the nearest pump or plant.
I rarely if ever found a clog, so I now wonder
if my days as a professional turd herder
might have been more about hazing
a college kid than needed reconnaissance.

Not that I really minded the job, after all
it paid well enough, and once I learned
to hold my breath as I jerked the cover open,
it really wasn't that terrible of a gig.
I got to work alone, well except for the flies,
and I learned all I ever needed to know
to hold any other job that I bumbled into
which is mainly that the shit always runs
downhill and when things go wrong,
you need to watch your step, and stay out
of the crap, so you don't bring it home.

The Builder of Better Angel Dance Floors

Home from college, one summer weekend
with not much to do, I went to a local bar
with my dad. When he left his stool to piss,
Goo Goo, Crazy Joe, and Lumpy, his co-workers
and union brothers, sidled over to educate me.
"Sport, your old man would kill us if he knew
we told you this, but you should know,
your father is the best damn welder in the local.
They say Al Berecka could weld the heads
of two pins together." They all shook their heads
in agreement and skedaddled back to their stools
once the men's room door swung open.
As he reclaimed his seat my dad asked,
"What was that about?" "Ah, nothing,"
I said as the other men nodded knowingly,
and I tried to hide any hint of admiration.
Just as someone asked, "So who's buying
the next round?" and the bar settled back
to its proper business—washing down pride.

Alan Gann *facilitates after-school programming and writing workshops for under-served youth at Texans Can Academies. He is the author of three volumes of poetry including* Better Ways to See *(2022 from Assure Press),* That's Entertainment, *and* Adventures of the Clumsy Juggler. *He also wrote* DaVerse Works *a performance poetry curriculum.*

Southern White Boy Prayer

bless aching muscles
plowed same stingy acres
year after year and hauled
fifty-pound bags
from over there to over here
understanding
never be enough
end-of-the-month
wallets and soup still grow thin
rent looms large

bless the bossman
who always fills his quota
just before I break

and bless tar-stained cap
worn all summer
working on Mr. Jackson's
tobacco farm
snapping suckers
priming ripest fields
hanging leaves

yes
bless the tractor supply cap
living on the shelf
above my desk

amazed
I get to sit in
air-conditioned cube
sending out reports
nobody will ever read

Dwarf #1 – Grumpy

what was once chilly
now just cold cold cold
snow day just another way to say
hi ho hi ho
no work no pay no romance
left for fluffy powder
falling from above
because I am well acquainted
with ill-intentioned ice and love
and knees rather complain
than move another ton of rock
for wages wouldn't feed a mouse
so's I drink
perhaps a drop more than I should
only thing still feels good
going down when even sitting
becomes a chore
incomplete without grunt and groan
and could you speak up
just a little
not that anybody's actually listening
I know I know I know
more than I understand
and understand things I could
never know
somedays I am experienced
and others just old old old

Dickson, Tennessee 1935

As the stationmaster, Grandpa swept the floor, unlocked
the doors, sold the tickets, and hired the bulls that beat
those who jumped the trains.

X inside a circle and stick figure cat scribed beside the
backyard gate welcomed weary wanderers.

Every Sunday when they got home from church, two pint
jars of shine waited just inside the screen door for never
specified medicinal purposes.

Trunk beside the mulberry stained picnic table held
clothes collected by ladies of the Eastern Star.

If he drank enough, Grandpa didn't dream the howls of
hobos thrown from rolling boxcars of fingers snapped
like twigs.

Coal dusted men pumped cool water from the well,
washed faces and hands, filled mugs, and sat quietly at the
table— knew to keep eyes cast downward.

Grandpa stood on the platform and watched the Klan
march round his station. Wouldn't let nobody in less they
removed their hood, so none of the porters were beaten
that day.

On Saturday after locking up the station Grandpa would
stop by Fossie's pit for a pound of the best pulled pork
tween Memphis and Gatlinburg.
Grandma fried up slabs of corn pone and kept a kettle of
beans simmering.

Eye or cheek sometimes bruised, dress soaked with sweat,
Fossie always smiled while counting out his change.

When pay train arrived from Nashville on Friday afternoon without enough money in the bags, they divided up what was there and made do.

Grandma served them all the same, said hunger was a color-blind bulldog who didn't care noways.

Nothing he could do when four drunks whipped the watermelon man's son for a cheeky smile flashed at shopkeeper's daughter.

And every Sunday Grandpa promised the Lord that if he lived long enough to retire, he would never touch that shine again.

Angela Hooper *has lived in Oklahoma City all of her life and has written poetry since she was 12. She received her BA in English from the University of Central Oklahoma. Her affiliation with the Individual Artists of Oklahoma helped to build her craft as she read her own work and helped host monthly readings. She has published in* The Mom Egg, Crosstimbers, *and the* Woody Guthrie anthology, Ain't Gonna Be Treated This Way. *She lives with her husband of 20 years and their teenage daughter.*

Being Working Class 2023

There is the routine
Minds that pull
Bodies upward
Repetition of days on days
Wild exotic puppets
Looking for a space
To move electric
Away from the parts
Of our bodies
That live in pain.

I wonder about the propensity
How much movement
Can you produce
In the allotted time
Mandated by jealous budgets
That cut hours
From those who
Can least afford
To lose the shifts.

it's about the velocity

That has taken over
The hidden factories
Where we work
With the expectations
That hands and minds
Are as fast
As the computers
That confine us
To unsustainable margins
Excising those
Who have lost the bet.

Annmarie Lockhart *is the founding editor of* vox poetica, *an online poetry salon, and* Unbound Content, *an independent poetry press. A New Jersey resident, she lives and writes two miles east of the hospital where she was born. You can read her words in fine journals online and in print.*

15 Potentialities When Learning About Tipping

Should you find yourself driving with your sleepless baby and your semi-retired dad and you get a flat tire, here is what might happen:

1. A random man might stop to help.
2. He might spend some time talking to your dad, who will likely share his gold standard car maintenance tips: never let the gas tank drop below three-quarters and never skip the carwash when you fill the tank.
3. You will, no doubt, tip the man, who will then drive out of your story and into someone else's.
4. Unexpectedly, your dad might then ask: *What the hell was that?* to which you'd probably answer: *A tip?*
5. If your dad pressed the question: *You just handed him $20 bucks?* you might think you'd mis-stepped: *Too much? Too little?*
6. You'd likely be confused if he answered: *You don't just hand someone a tip. That's not the right way to do it.*
7. And it could be that you would ask: *Well, what's the right way to do it?*
8. It would make sense, at this point, for you to consider your dad's background: Born in Antwerp in 1924, drawn to the Resistance when the Nazis

rolled into Belgium, put to work when he got caught.

9. It would also make sense for you think about his eventual migration to New Jersey, his decades of service in a small-town Department of Public Works, and his rise to the rank of Chief in the local fire department, the way he married your mom and gained two daughters, you and your sister, who reminded him of the stray cats that perpetually flocked to his door.

10. At this point, it would also do you good to remember some of the lessons this man (fluent in 5 languages despite an 8th-grade education) taught you:

> a. Stupid decisions sometimes have good outcomes, but that doesn't make you smart, it makes you lucky.
>
> b. Any job you had is the best job you have.
>
> c. That one about sleeping with the dog and getting his fleas.
>
> d. Money is unreliable but joy is worth a gamble.
>
> e. That one about the cow and the free milk.
>
> f. Hard work doesn't guarantee a reward but there's no point working any other way.

11. By now, you might be half-prepared to hear him say: *You throw the money on the floor and you walk away so he can pick it up after you leave.*

12. Still, no one would blame you if you asked: *What if he doesn't see me throw it on the floor and he thinks I didn't tip him?*

13. Who among us would expect him to answer: *Then he's a jerk! But that's not the point.*

14. Bewilderment might creep into your voice if you
asked: *What's the point of throwing money on the
ground?*
15. You'd be forgiven for having no words if he
answered: *If you make a man open his palm to
you like he's a beggar and you're the fucking
Queen of Sheba, you're not tipping him, you're
robbing him. Of his dignity.*

Mercy Plays the Long Game

A working man knocked up his girlfriend in
Dublin in 1941. He found himself at the mercy of
the Sisters of Mercy and in exchange for that mercy,
he paid his penance in pounds rather than Hail Marys.

The man worked to send what he could
to the Sisters of Mercy, who felt it was a mercy
to take his money and keep his son, the one he had
loved since the first and only time he had held him.

The working man and his girlfriend did not find mercy
in remembering the curve of their son's cheek, the
grip of his hand, the down of his newborn hair.
She left for America, to a new life with a new name

and he left for work in London, where he would
become a bereft shadow, drowning his grief and rage
in the mercy of the bottle. It might've been a genuine
mercy when he died, too young and alone.

The working man would never know the mercy of
learning his son would one day paint his life and the
stories of starved babies and the parents from whom
they were stolen by the merciful Sisters of Mercy.

The working man would never know the mercy of being found by the forced foundling who painted no mercy into his colors for the Sisters of Mercy. But it would be something if he did, perhaps, find peace.

Maybe those paintings by the son of that working man from Dublin will resonate with other working men and their children. And maybe one day we will learn the meaning of mercy and unlock the promise of Eden.

Borrowed Words

(with thanks to John Lewis, Charles Dickens,
Woody Guthrie, Thomas Jefferson, and
the Dropkick Murphys)

> I was not concerned about my body.
> No one was going to kill my soul.
> —John Lewis
> *Walking With the Wind:*
> *A Memoir of a Movement*

Dickens warned us about Ignorance
and Want but many among us worship both.

A year ago we saw a small man with old bombs
attempt to pillage an ancient nation.

And since we notched a million extra dead, labor held
a winning hand, but lost it. The house always wins.

Every year we train fewer minds and fewer hands
to redesign the old ideas we dust off for BBQs.

When AI and the chatbots take over, we'll need
an army to reconstruct this American experiment.

It's always the writers that remind us which of those
revolutionary truths we still hold to be self-evident.

Poets, it's time to raise the alarm again, to shout
the calls to action for another generation

to come meet us where the trouble's at
not once, not twice, but ten times more,

til we congregate, again, in the shadow of giants
with blood on our collars but courage

in our hearts, our spirits unconcerned about
the condition of our bodies,

not once, not twice, but ten times more
and ten times more, and ten times ten times more.

Barbara Shepherd, *award-winning poet/writer/artist, is a Woody Guthrie Poet, Poetry Society of Oklahoma's Poet Laureate, State of Oklahoma Poet Laureate Nominee, and Oklahoma State Fair's Voice of the Fair Poet. She wrote* Vittles and Vignettes, Patchwork Skin, River Bend, *and* The Potbelly Pig Promise. *Her poems are in* Woody's Travelin' Music, Elegant Rage, *and* Ain't Gonna Be Treated This Way, *and in other anthologies and poetry journals.* www.barbarashepherd.com

Working Hands

Grandpa Hopkins never complained about his
hands, but they must have pained him.
Oversized knuckles and fingers knotted like tree
stumps made it difficult for him to shuffle cards.
He managed, jamming them into each other in the
deck, and licking his thick thumb often as he dealt,
because playing Pitch was as much a Sunday
afternoon tradition as fried chicken at noon.

Gentle and loving, those hands had held his babies,
and later, their babies.
He had gripped a belt for discipline,
hoes to chop cotton,
reins of leather to drive mules,
and hammer and nails to build a WPA bridge.
His hands served him well at the card table,
but the old man wasn't done for the day.

Softball called his name, and all ages played.
Patient kids waited as he struggled with shoelaces.
He untied his old work boots of cordovan,
blistered and scuffed to a tan.
He shed them and his red-heeled-monkey socks
before he grabbed the weathered baseball bat.
He hit a long drive and ran barefoot
over sandburs in the pasture,

tagging bases of scrap wood
in his faded overalls and floppy hat,
clapping his gnarled hands
when he scored at home plate.

Years of hard work to support a big family
through the Depression and two wars
showed in his hands. His love of family did, too.

Cutting Wood

Nothing hampers our quest
for firewood – the fuel we crave
come winter's fury.
Traipsing past the cow lot and pig pens,
almost as silent as the snow blanketing them,
Daddy and I reach the woods.

I get to mark the trees we'll cut down.
Daddy wields the chainsaw like a lumberjack,
frightening the birds who had not flown south.
I carry the short logs and stack them.
When we can boast two ricks, I gather twigs
for kindling, and we head home
for a roaring fire and hot cocoa.

The Balladeer

They call him the voice of injustice
as he champions the working man.

But a sudden fall robs him of speech.
Fully clothed, he is naked without words.

News of his silence ripples through the crowd.

They form a circle for his poems of protest.
Nothing escapes his wordless lips.
Now as silent as he, they watch him pick up
his guitar and strum a familiar rhythm.
His eyes close until the world he knows goes black.
Thoughts of a life without song tear at his brain.

His unexpected scream jars everyone
but returns him to his destiny.
Leaping upon a red sandstone,
he sings the message he carries in his heart.

Bill McCloud *is a poetry editor for the* Right Hand Pointing *literary journal and is the poetry reviewer for* Vietnam Veterans of America. *His poetry book,* The Smell of the Light, *published by Balkan Press, reached #1 on The Oklahoman's "Oklahoma Bestsellers" list. His poems have appeared in* Oklahoma Today *and the* Oklahoma English Journal, *and dozens are taught at the University School of Milwaukee, WI, the University of Tulsa, and the Air Force Academy.*

Work Boots

As a young child my
dad's work boots
always seemed to
transport him to
a different world

One where he worked
high up in the oil refinery
as high as you could go

The boots used for walking
to work in the snow because
he didn't believe we lived far
enough away for him to drive

Boots he put on that time
he volunteered to go to a nearby
town and spent a week repairing
tornado-damaged roofs of
people he didn't even know

Evenings we played together
Watched TV threw a ball around
But next morning he would put
those work boots back on and go
to some place that also

seemed to bring him joy

Because it's the smile I remember
The one he always left for work with
The one he was still wearing when
he came home at the end of the day.

Denim Shirts

We never quite made it
to that white-collar world.
It's those blue denim shirt wearin'
folks who still keep things movin'
you know. Eliminate most of
those white-collar jobs and
we'd probably still be okay
But try to remove the blue collar
ones and I'm not too sure
where we'd go from there But I
believe we'd get there pretty fast.

The Only Thing

The money in a working man's
check lasts exactly as long as it
takes for the next one to arrive.
His energy lasts exactly as long
as it takes to finish the job.
His love for his family
may be the only thing in
his life that is limitless.

Cassie Premo Steele, *Ph.D., is a lesbian, ecofeminist, mother, poet, novelist, and essayist whose writing focuses on the themes of trauma, healing, creativity, mindfulness and the environment. She is an award-winning author of 16 books and audio programs ranging from novels to poetry and nonfiction and scholarship. Her newest book,* Swimming in Gilead, *is forthcoming from Yellow Arrow Publishing in 2023. Her website www.cassiepremosteele.com*

The Year of Lists

We wrote lists of groceries and things
we needed for the house and skin,
lists of chores to complete, reminders
of calls to make and things to take in,
lists of medicines and their times,
symptoms and their intensity,
lists of memories we almost forgot
that came back to us in the night.

We wrote lists until we didn't, when
everything went online, even shopping
happened without handwriting,
the toilet paper and the lotion lying
next to the apples and rice on the porch,
the medicines coming in the mail,
the chores suddenly pared down to
dusting and the endless dishes.

We wrote lists in our head then,
restaurants we missed, people
we'd kissed who were now dead,
until the lists got so long that we had
to erase daily what had gone wrong,
we had to press our palms against
the screen and call this love and work,
blending friendship and collegiality.

We wrote lists again after some time,
released like inmates from our own
homes, and once more picking up
dog food seemed like a necessary
chore to do, and we wondered how
many of our neighbors who were
still alive had been sick, and we prayed
at every sniffle and allergy and flu.

We wrote lists of what mattered when,
after a whiskey or two, late at night,
we were no longer alone: breath,
trust, touch, laughter, breath again—
and our tears came down then
like a list of all we could not say,
like what was here one day and
gone the next. Gone, gone away.

Let Us Let Go

Let us let go of stuff, the art we kept out of
fear or status, the junk, post-it notes and
reminders to self that are on an app now,
the books we read once and didn't love,
or never read and never want to, the presents
and cards that meant something at the time,
the things your mother gave you to keep
because she no longer wanted them,
but you don't really either, the notes from
classes you don't need because you've taught
them so many times you can do it in your
sleep, the envelopes you thought you'd use,
the free bookmarks: how many bookmarks
can you really use at once anyway?

And

keep these:

photos, how little they were, how young you
were, how classy they were, how afraid you
were, how happy they were, how
inexperienced about everything you were.

　　　The journals, arranged by year, peek
inside just long enough to remember the
seasons: depression, dissertation,
motherhood, striving, love, learning,

　　　　　　　　　　and eventually leaving
each one behind.

Let us let go of the year even as we embrace

what is no longer here: the dead who still care,
the work that is done, the dreams we had and
woke from, the selves we were on the way to
becoming a completely new one.

Flower, Fly, Catch

i. flower

I was an orange lotus bed, a bed
for bodies to rest and be blessed,
make love and make life. There was beauty in
the shining light of my closed petals, the veins
ran through with liquid that was warm and
sighed.

But I was not open. I was tight. As lovely as
that flower was, it was frozen. Afraid, still,
made so by what might happen again
that had once long ago happened and I'd
worked so hard to relieve and release and
relax and it was all hard, hard work, great
trying, and never really letting go or letting in

22

or letting be.

It was an internal mountain I forged all by myself, daily, and I told myself I didn't need a sherpa, I was fine all by myself.

ii. fly

I could fly. I'd learned to whizz by with my wings in glittering iridescence, I could go forward and backward and make loops and figure eights, and the shapes of my flight drew all kinds of astonishing things.

Until I fell. And flat on my back, my tail feathers en masse and my beak overturned, I lay there, wondering why this had happened and the pain was so great, and I could not even move, and all of the trying was useless.

iii. catch

It was one of my own petals, I realized, that caught me.

Catherine Katey Johnson *is an award-winning poet, writer, published author, and artist whose works are included in films, textbooks, anthologies, literary journals and chapbooks. A Woody Guthrie Poet, a* BEAT *poet,* Cowboy Poet, *and* Oklahoma Poet, *she is degreed from Rose State and* UCO. *Her collections are* Fifty Shades of Gray Hair, a tangled collection *and* Resting Soil, *neither of which have numbered pages because in Oklahoma women don't count.*

Loaned Twenty-twos

Betty loaned me Twenty-five today.
"It was found money," she said
and she would get it back, she knew,
when I made it.
Yes, she would, I said, as she drove us to the coffeehouse.

The Redcup then was
three
for soup and bread for one.
That makes twenty-two.

She let me out at my door,
and a few hours later there was a knock.
John, from up the street.
His daughter's parole officer
had informed him that she could not live
in a place which had any weapons
so he brought it tenderly down
to my house, wrapped in a swaddling blanket
held gently together with two masking tape straps
a papoose for his rifle.

He would not store his other weapons
the ones he uses on us both:
belittling and judgement; the constant demeaning
and a look of doubt for any dream uttered,
then a quick change of subject;

blank stares to the side when you talk of reaching goals
or honors bestowed by Higher-Ed
or publication credits.
John? I say.

He looks back, sighs and breathes.
"Well. That's nice, I guess," he replies,
and thinks that that will do it.

Those weapons he keeps close to his side
and in fast draw readiness.
While he keeps me here,
across the street and him over there
out of target range
with his .22 stored under my bed
and me, with twenty-two to my name.

You're Supposed to Go Commando with a Ghi

Well, she wasn't quite old
but she was going through the change
and she never knew when or where
it would kick in.
Her "Visit from her Aunt from America,"
as her German friend called the curse,
could be heavy or light and last a day or a few.
So, it was always good to use a tampon, just in case.
Especially, if one was exercising, or doing Yoga,
or Karate Class outdoors in the park in Nichols Hills.

That day, they were working on their kicks:
a half-hour of exercise, followed by running laps, and
stretches.
Then, on to Bunkais, Kumites and thirty minutes of
kicks.

25

Forward kicks all the way across the park and back.
Then side left, then side right, and finally, across the field
and back with the powerful round-house kick.
First right. Then left.

When she got home, she went to shower and change her
tampon, but it wasn't there.
It was when she started the class.
Gone now.

She decided it was just easier not to ever go back to
Karate.
Besides, she had developed the ultimate weapon.
A round-house kick with a flying braided-tail surprise
smack to the forehead.

Those Low Down, Low-Key, Low-Life Society Blues

This here song's for my new old friend
I'm just sittin' here singin' it out,
Hopin' that my heart is gonna' mend.
Well, I been singin' so long
That I damn near sung up every song.
So I'm writin' just one more song,
For my new old friend.

Oh, I've got those low down, low-key,
low-life society blues.
I've been shuffle-steppin' out of the past,
'til I wore down both the soles of my shoes.
Well, just one look at me, and you can plainly see
my woes outweigh my woos.
I've got them low down, low-key, low-life society blues.

I left home and I was about thirty

a boozed and cruised, and squandered my cash
And my love life, dang, it made me feel dirty
I called my 82-year-old Columbian granny
to see if she could take me in.
but she said no, and it's a cryin' sin.
Then she hung up and went into labor
and had a forty-year-old calcified baby.

Oh, I've got those low down, low-key,
low-life society blues.
I've been shuffle-steppin' out of the past,
'til I wore down both the soles of my shoes.
Well, just one look at me, and you can plainly see
my woes outweigh my woos.
I've got them low down, low-key, low-life society blues.

So I thumbed it out to somewhere near Porum
(Oklahoma) and I fell in a frozen pond
I crawled out baptized, naked, no decorum
And an empty case that once held my bass
Became a bed for my shivering body to place
Then they took me to jail
'cause I was naked and pale.

Oh, I've got those low down, low-key,
low-life society blues.
I've been shuffle-steppin' out of the past,
'til I wore down both the soles of my shoes.
Well, just one look at me, and you can plainly see
My woes outweigh my woos.
I've got them low down, low-key, low-life society blues.

Well this here verse, may be my worst.
But if tears could measure my emotions,
You could damn near fill up all of the oceans!
I just keep on tryin' but all I get is lyin'
Then I start cryin'

'cause I got those low down, low-key, low-life society
blues, yeah!

Refrain:
Oh, I've got those low down, low-key, low-life society
blues.
I've been shuffle-steppin' out of the past,
'til I wore down both the soles of my shoes.
Well, just one look at me, and you can plainly see
My woes outweigh my woos.
I've got them low down, low-key, low-life society blues.

Christopher Carmona *is an award-winning author and a member of the award-winning* Refusing to Forget *project. His novel,* El Rinche: The Ghost Ranger of the Rio Grande, *was a finalist for the 2019 Best Young Adult Novel for the Texas Institute of Letters. His short story collection,* The Road to Llorona Park, *won the 2016 NACCS Tejas Best Fiction Award and was listed as one of the top 8 Latinx books in 2016 by NBC News. He served on Responsible Ethnic Studies Textbook committee that was awarded the "float like a butterfly, sting like a bee" award for excellence in educational leadership from the Mexican American School Board Association (MASBA). He is also an inductee to the Texas Institute of Letters*

Everything Belongs To Me

everything belongs to me.
I am poor.
every language belongs to me.
I am colonized.
every song belongs to me.
I am silenced.
every food belongs to me.
I am hungry.
every border divides me.
I am the land.
every hour belongs to me.
time cannot keep my story.

Little Windows

Sprinkled throughout South Texas cafes
mostly old Tex Mex joints
where you pay at a cash register
surrounded by Mexican candies
& an assortment of tiny Jesus' & Virgins

Behind the nice cashier
is a small sliding window

"Is that for take out?"
"Si y no."
That little window had always been there.
A remnant from a time forgotten
when Mexicans couldn't eat inside
they had to use the little window...

Ours Is a History

Our is a history told in a house without windows
written not from what survives
but from what is lost...

Theirs is a history told in a house without mirrors
written without ever once looking at themselves
as they took an eraser to us...
.

Cullen Whisenhunt *is a graduate of Oklahoma City University's Red Earth Creative Writing MFA program whose work has appeared in* Dragon Poet Review, The Bamboo Hut, *and* The Ekphrastic Review, *among other journals. He has published two chapbooks with Fine Dog Press,* Among the Trees *(2020) and* Childish Thing and Other Experiments *(2023) and was a 2022 Guthrie Poet.*

Too Poor To Get Sick

After "I Ain't Got No Home," by Woody Guthrie

Can't afford no healthcare,

so I've had to go without
This COVID's got me scared,
but my constitution's stout.
My boss man's done gone home
and I'm working all his shifts,
So I hope I dodge the virus,
'cause I'm too poor to get sick.

Well, the whole world's staying home now
all to keep from getting ill,
But my landlord won't let up,
just keeps piling on the bills,
So my hands, they both stay busy
stuffing pockets for the rich.
Man, I hope I dodge the virus,
'cause I'm too poor to get sick.

Now, I'm working nights and weekends
in this groc'ry check-out line,
Havin' close contact with people,
'bout a hundr'd at a time,
But I know this work's "essential,"
so I'm here through thin and thick.
I just hope I dodge the virus,
'cause I'm too poor to get sick.

I'm worried 'bout my parents
and I'm worried 'bout my kids.
I don't think that we could pay it
if they came down with COVID.
Plus, there's millions go untreated
for a lack of testing kits,
So I hope I dodge the virus,
'cause I'm too poor to get sick.

Now as I look around,
it's a-mighty plain to see
This world is such a strange
and a funny place to be.
Oh, the working men stay poor
while the lay-abouts stay rich,
And we still can't catch no breaks,
'cause we're too poor to get sick.

Crossable

Swollen and red
like an enlarged artery,
the Washita River
flexes against its bank,
pushing the greens of life
further into themselves.

Soon, its silted current
will abrade bark, bank,
and bridge alike, scouring
the black of burnt rubber
and charred asphalt from the road
just west of Ravia, where life's worst
accidents all seem to assemble:
colleagues, gone in a moment of screeching;

uncles, lost in a lifetime of bad decisions;
grandmothers, killed by a lifetime of only one. But,

still or not, the river will be forded,
for much of normality lies on the other side:
professions, friendships, weekend groceries,
each an impetus and product
of the crossing.

So rage on, mud river, rise
with the rains and run rampant,
waylaying the living and erasing
the detritus of the dead.

To misquote Ginsberg,
"while you're here,
I'll do the work,"
and I like a challenge.

Daryl Ross Halencak *is a rural poet. Readers can find out about him and his latest collection,* Raw and Personal without Apology *at atomicbombpoetry.com*

Freedom

I'm tired.
I'm thirsty.
Give me a drink before I die.
My mouth is parched-dry as a bone like desert sands.
Let me sit beneath a shade tree and rest from my yoke.
Heavy and broken,
I labor underneath your repression.
I'm a slave,
and I'm slaking for freedom.

We are Sharecroppers

men in fields
sweating from heat
without water
longs for supper time
ready for bed
the day had been heavy
struggling for the fall
harvest
summer sun sucks up all
moisture
with heads bowed and eyes closed
the family prayed to survive
crops
dad and his dad
before tending plowed clay
armpits smell like hard work
without a stock tank for swimming or bathing

damn greedy
Carpetbaggers stole our lands
sharecroppers-that's who we are.

D.L. Lang *is an internationally published poet and poet laureate emerita of Vallejo, California. She is a member of the Revolutionary Poets Brigade San Francisco and the IWW Printers & Publisher's Union #450. She has performed at demonstrations, festivals, and poetry shows across California. She grew up in many places, including Enid, Oklahoma. Find her at poetryebook.com*

Together We Will Rise

From the indigenous workers robbed of their land,

to the Black workers forced to pick and build this land,
to the Latino migrants kept from traveling this land,
to the Chinese workers who built our railroads,
to the Japanese workers unfairly interned,
to the Arab workers falsely accused of violence,
to the Jewish workers who escaped fascist hands,
to the Irish workers who fled a divided homeland,
to the queer workers forced to hide who they love,
to the trans workers forced to hide their true souls,
to the women workers forced to labor in their homes,
to the children who work for low wages in sweatshops,
to the working poor forced to live in outright squalor,
to the homeless people who must beg for a dollar,
to the disabled workers who are grossly underpaid,
to the incarcerated workers seeking mercy and freedom,
to the brave union workers who died in labor struggles,
to the workers injured by war, police, and the draft,
we have so much in common with one another.
One day we'll unite to take back what's rightfully ours
from those who exploited, bombed, and divided the
people.
For centuries now the rich have committed a great evil.
When we get together there's no stopping what's in store.
On that great day all of us will settle the score,

flipping this world together for justice and peace
once more!

You Lot That Cause This Rot

You lot born into multi-millions
who plunder wealth from the workers' hands,
while destroying every inch of our land.
You who see us as beneath you—
we who work our hands to the bone
to fund your billion dollar homes,
your collections of silver and gold,
your private jets and idle time—
your time's end will surely come
for we outnumber you a million to one,
and this upside down world is getting old.
It's the greatest evil you've unfurled.
You wouldn't last a day in our shoes.
A single second would give you the blues.
We built everything across this world,
only for you to take it from our hands,
denying us a livelihood and health plans.
You enslave us to the time clock,
say no to every reasonable request
for flexibility, accommodation,
or precious time with family.
One day we'll put you to the test.
Freedom is our human right,
and the time is long overdue
for us to finish up this fight
by wrestling what we built
from your soft greedy hands,
so humanity can flourish in every land.

No Greater Love

Working folks trudge and toil
until we're all used up,
discarded before our prime
never reaping the spoils
inside the rich man's cup,
but if workers ran the world,
we wouldn't have to worry
for all of life would spark our glory.
If working folks ran the world,
we'd pay people above their worth
no matter the job large or small,
so every human could stand tall.
If working folks ran the world,
we'd have more time to enjoy
all the people that we adore
instead of missing out more.
If working folks ran the world,
it would cease to run on greed.
Life wouldn't be about what got sold.
Everyone'd have exactly what they need.
The world would turn on love not gold.
If working folks ran the world,
we'd make sure our neighbors,
every one, were properly housed
with enough food for every mouth.
No one would ever again go without.

If working folks ran the world,
it'd be a big union of humanity
filled with love for you and me
for there's no greater love
than our eternal solidarity.

Hank Jones *did not send me a bio, so I shall provide the one I used to introduce him last year, when he also did not provide me with a bio: There are some who suspect Hank Jones is Batman; this sells him short. Batman, in fact, has a Hank Jones Signal. The World's Most Interesting Man calls Hank for Interesting Advice. Waldo looks for him. Wordle posts daily its Hank score. He is the "G" in GPS the "carte" in "a la carte" and the "mode" in "a la mode." He is also a damn fine poet and author of* Too Late for Manly Hands *(2021 Turning Plow Press)*

Digging a Grave

I helped dig a grave with some ranchers
one of whose boys had died.
Mentally disabled, he had drowned in a swimming pool
when everyone else looked away.
The father, in his grief,
built his son's casket of unfinished pine,
then we joined him to dig the grave.
There were eight or ten of us, boys and men,
taking turns with a metal rod to break up the
hard New Mexico soil,
then one by one, we'd jump in the hole
and shovel out dirt
until our muscles ached
and we could no longer
lift the dirt-full shovel.
Then another would take a turn,
digging down as the hole got deeper.
Before too long, we were over our heads in the grave,
six by four.
It occurred to me as I worked
that this is the right way
to bury someone you love:
ache and sweat out the grief,
as the blisters form on your uncalloused hands.

My Season in Hell

I stick my hands in each pocket, looking
for things that stain, shred
or otherwise derail the process:

pocket change, lipstick, nails,
            wads of paper, chewing gum,
                        odd bits of this and that . . .
cologne, perfume, sweat,
            blood, urine, feces, cum . . .

Buttons on the left side in one pile,
            buttons on the right in another,
                        $1.50 for a shirt, $2.75 for a blouse,

pants, skirts, dresses, suits, neckties, scarves . . .

As long as the front door is open,
            the piles never shrink:
search the pockets, tag the stains, put them in piles,
            again and again and again.

I start to look at customers with hate,
            but it's a job, and it's the easy one,
keeps me out of the burning pits
            of perchloroethylene hell

where the unlucky ones live,
            stooped over steaming presses
perpetually from dark to midday
            when it'll be so hot outside,

leaving hell will be no relief.

The difference between me and those stuck in the back
        is that I'm young and a college student,
                and this is a part-time job,
and someday I'll leave this place behind forever,

but they'll remain
        until drugs or alcohol or immigration
                or some crime as yet unpunished

will sink them lower than they already are
        as they labor to make us unwrinkled and stain-
free.

Too Late for Manly Hands

I look at the fingers holding this page,
and I realize these are the hands I'll die with.

I always wanted the hands of working men,
carpenters and cowboys, plumbers and stonemasons,
rugged, brown, covered with tiny white scars,
capable of handling tools requiring strength:
hammers, lassos, wrenches.

My father's hands, my grandfather's,
men raised on farms and ranches,
men capable of wielding mighty tools.

I watched my father hammer steel posts with a
sledgehammer
deep into the earth while I held the steel beam, cowering,
as he rared back with each mighty swing
and brought the hammer down perfectly, every time,

always certain one day he'd miss and drive the hammer
into my too soft head,
Abraham needlessly killing Isaac while God looked on
promising nothing.

The work of reading and grading that I do now
does nothing to challenge my hands.

I think of Seamus Heaney and his pen
and know that his poem was really about shame,
shame that he was not the man his fathers were,

just a poet, weakened by the need to sit inside
and read and write,
doing what has to be done.

But something in us rebels,
rails angrily against the choices we have made,
demands that we head outdoors and prove our manhood
in the old ways of righteous labor.

And though we know this thinking is wrong,
that the world does not respond to
or take note of its laborers,
that if we want to make a difference, it will be words,
and words alone
that will get us heard,

still, it doesn't sit right somehow
and my hands stand in accusation against me.

James Thomas Fletcher *is native to Oklahoma. After a brief stint in college, he left the state to see if the rest of the world existed. Along the way, he picked cotton, made fiberglass and, in hazmat suit, cleaned filters inside a nuclear laundry. He was an M-60 machine gunner in the Central Highlands of Vietnam, company clerk at Supreme Headquarters Allied Powers Europe, (NATO\ SHAPE) in Belgium, bartender in South Carolina, bricklayer in Oklahoma, oil field chainhand in Louisiana, roustabout in the Gulf of Mexico, English instructor in North Carolina, and Director of Computer-Aided Instruction at the University of Illinois in Chicago. After living on the side of a volcano in the Republic of Panamá, he recently returned to the red dirt prairie of Oklahoma.*

Before I Was Born

Before I was born my grandparents' house
had two front doors and a wheelchair ramp.
I never saw either even in photos
but I remember them. I remember them
from the stories, the questions I asked.

I picture great-grandma Rachel rocking
in a rocking chair on that front porch though
more than likely she would be in her wheelchair.
I remember. She looks out across the street, still
dirt back then. The yellow stop sign not yet up.

A row of iris lines street and walk. Gray-green,
never blooming, perennially coated with dust.
Beside the path for drive, a catalpa tree
suspends stiletto beanpod swords of Damocles.
Does she miss the lush Tennessee of her youth?

Yards are open. The Drydens had some hog
wire for a horse. My grandparents had chicken
wire for a coop out back. In the 60s, the Spencers
put up a chain-link around front. My dad did

our backyard for the dogs. But all that was later.

I remember a mule team passing our house,
rented out to pull stumps. I remember the train
passing, trying to run those two blocks before
it passed. I remember Hudson Hornets and trees
darkening the street on that eerie end.

On that end the twins lived. And the German
war bride. And the kid with polio. Somehow
those two blocks to the tracks were mysterious.
The witch's house was there, vines snaking
all over with a dark touch of age, and sinister.

Before I was born the neighborhood was quiet.
Tin Lizzies replaced with soft bulbous shapes
moving sparsely along in their hum of power.
No one had gasoline mowers. Reel mowers cut
grass in silence, the sound of scissors snipping.

Like the barber shop grandpa had out back before
it became a corner store. Everyone knows a dollar
is too much, his business card read. I remember
that shop I never saw. And the tall grass growing
in places before houses. Fields with turtles.

Crawdads in creeks that somehow later vanished.
Oil wells pumping silently twenty-four hours a day.
In the 60s a church was built on that spot.
The Spencers were dead then. And the Drydens.
Mr. Shaw still riding his bike with fat tires.

Before I was born the TV was black and white
and no one had one. Kids all had new transistors
and they wouldn't work. Telephones were always black.
Stick your finger in a hole and pull. Long distance
was expensive and never used. Numbers were short.

44

Bathrooms moved into the house before I was born.
Your pantry is probably larger than the bath
my dad built for our family of six back when
it was a family of three. That's me, there,
the third, arriving before my siblings.

Gas open flames warm the bathroom. Glowing
ceramic. Wall heater, floor heater.
Long counterbalance bolts of iron
hung from rope inside
every wooden window frame.

Transoms above the door. Beneath
the house, in the dim, dark, shadowy,
cobwebby cellar, shelves of jars, summer's
abundance canned for winter. Creeks
of light with smudges of dust motes.
The kitchen creaks from being tacked on.
I watch grandma make vats of chicken 'n dumplings.
Grandpa drinking coffee, offering me sips
from his saucer. Oilskin tablecloth,
linoleum floor, cast iron everything.

They pull me back to that time I remember
and I don't remember but see so clearly.

I Am A Bricklayer

My hands are calloused
from the bark
of brick, the furrows of the palm
stained with mortar dye
the powder from every
sack of cement clogs my pores.

I crawl behind the wheel
my boots caked with morning mud
and imagine the comfort and quiet of home
the embrace and taste of her flesh
pulse of the shower
the sigh of warm socks on wet toes
and awaken to the distant tinkling
of pans and moist aromas
like the back of a Cairo café.

No longer am I tied to the day
tomorrow the ache
in my back will have dulled
tonight I do not commit suicide
by hangover, tonight
my mind is free
to glow like the orange halo
of the kiln
where bricks are born.

Cool Mountain Water

We walk along the mountain trail
beside a pleasant brook.
About twenty of us, teenagers mostly,
strolling beneath the green-dark canopy
providing shade and cooling
as we peramble the easy terrain.

My canteen is empty so I stop
to fill with cool water
when we ease for a break. I drop
in a purification tablet to kill
any unseen menace lurking
about and we continue our walk.

Within a hundred feet
around a small bend, we pass him.
The Viet Cong soldier.
Dead. Rotting. Decomposing.
Leaking ooze into the dark-green water
that I had poured like life into my canteen.

Jody Karr *is an author, artist, poet, and workshop instructor. Her art, poetry, and articles have been published in numerous publications. Jody's art has been exhibited in museums, galleries, national and international exhibits, and other venues. She lives on a half-acre in Oklahoma City with her animal family.*

Divided, But All One Sphere

Makeshift tents flap in the wind.
Men and women huddle.
Feet stomp, hands rub together.
I eye the stoplight,
lower a window.
My breath catches,
floats away on artic air.
Red-faced in a thin coat,
a man approaches.
I've no food or
money to give.
I roll up the blanket
beside me, reach out.
Our hands touch briefly.
He smiles, nods thanks,
then slips away into the
lengthening shadows.
The simple connection
warms me, ignites hope
for humanity, reminds me
we are divided, but all one sphere.

Joey Brown *is a poet and a fiction writer. She has authored two poetry collections:* The Feral Love Poems *(Hungry Buzzard Press) and* Oklahomaography *(Mongrel Empire Press). Her poems and prose have appeared in* The Red Earth Review, Plainsong, Concho River Review, Tulsa Review, Oklahoma Review, The San Pedro River Review, *and more. She frequently performs her poetry at festivals and writing conferences around the Midwest and sometimes beyond. Joey now lives in southwest Missouri with her husband, the novelist Michael Howarth. She and Michael were chosen as the featured writers of the Oswald Writers Series at the University of South Carolina-Aiken for 2023.*

Making a Hand

Where I come from, to make a hand
of yourself means you have done
something good,
something admirable.
Something to be pointed out
because people ought to know.
To make a hand shows strength,
character, sure. But grit,
stick-to-itiveness, a stretch
for the above and beyond,
unlikely to ever pay off in dollars,
likely to have to cost some pain.

It's not something to say often,
if I understand its application.
Take my father, for example.
Grew up around horses,
worked cattle,
and at rodeos,
and in oil and gas.

Hardly ever said it.
And if he ever did say it, it was
"There's somebody making
a hand of himself."
It caused the ears to prickle,
the eyes to look up,
the search for the one
stood outside the rest.

Think farm hand, ranch hand.
Think someone who picked cotton
and hauled hay before machines
did those things.
Think someone in a hard hat
standing roadside
smoothing asphalt
with a metal float
on a highway
in Southern Oklahoma
in July. There
was somebody
making a hand.

And if you saw that,
if you see it now,
That's a time you can speak
aloud the precious phrase,
mark someone's work with this distinction,
this compliment to be used sparingly.
This compliment that might be
the best someone could hope for.

Drought

When Marguerite gets up in the mornings now,
the subfloor bearing up the house her father
and grandfather built creaks brittle and dry,
as if the house might crack,
as if the house is giving up.
Marguerite fosters no blame.
Dues paid, old thing, she says out loud.

She pads down a hallway bigger than her kitchen,
cranks on the elderly coffee maker.
While she waits, she drifts through rooms,
shakes the fine grit that's settled overnight
from her papers and picture frames,
touches fingertips to the nail heads
popping through sheetrock.
New ones every day.

Marguerite travels the seasick slanting
of the shifted house to her patio,
a concrete slab cracked and rubbling
into grass no longer in need of mowing.
She sips, lets her eyes unfocus.
Her kids called last night to say,
again, she should move to town.
Before it's too late,
one of them finally said.
If they only knew.
When Marguerite brings herself
to look across the plain, she sees
her father, a combine, barbed wire
fencing, and a scraggly handful of cattle.
None there, of course, but every day
she looks for them, and every day

she finds them. Like a slice of sepia
toned 1940s film, the scene plays.
Her father and the cows with heads
bowed to the tree bending wind.

Marguerite blinks. Modern day sun,
too bright, explodes, and she goes back inside.
The tv weatherman says virga hangs
in the atmosphere above them.
Even a small shift in the jet stream means rain.
But he's been saying that for months now,
and when Marguerite looks up
she sees only a sky eating away
at the land of her horizon, below
that, the hairline fractures of her earth
covered by wildfire-eaten pastures.

Johnie Catfish *is a street poet in the OKC area and has been involved with poetry groups and readings across the state. He lives in Edmond with his patient wife and makes different forms of what he calls art.*

The Deal

I know I drew this Working Man's Hand
Some say "Hardest Damn Cards in the deck
And you just can't win with a losing hand.
But I'm going to hold my cards close.
And play them smart, cause I'm going all in.
Going to organize a union, stage a strike.
Marching and protesting until we get our rights.
Rights to good jobs with living wages,
Homes we can afford with dignity and respect.
No longer held down by poverty and neglect.
Let our voices rise up in this Land of Liberty,
The Working Man living proud and free with equality.

Working Man's Prayer

Lord, give me good honest work,
Fair pay, a boss that's not a jerk.
Keep me safe from hurt and harm.
And free from stupid bureaucracy.
As you give me mercy and grace
Help me pray for others in needs.

I pray for the farmers who are praying for rain,
Worrying about losing their land.
For the stiff neck Bankers being mean
Foreclosing on their neighbors' farms,
Afraid their banks just might fail.

For preachers sounding happy about the After Life
When they're not too sure about the here and now.
For the hobos and the homeless left
Going nowhere, hopeless, no one to care.
For the orphans, the abandoned, the old and the sick.
For the prisoners in prison, the guards with the stick.
For the cop on the beat, the kids in the streets.
For the soldiers on duty, their families at home.
For the waitresses, the cooks, the dishwashers too.
For the poets who lost the rhythm and rhyme.
There's not enough time, so little I can do
But help us all, Lord, to make it through.
Amen

What A Working Man Needs

Smart asses say I'm living check to check.
Keener eyes see I'm barely getting by,
Working hard just trying to make ends meet.
What's needed is a worthy task to have pride in,
A fair boss, letting me earn some respect,
Living wage so I can pay my own way,
And affordable house, having some dignity.

Got a strong back and willing heart and hands
To work hard, planning a better future
With my loving wife, raising our children
To always pray, stay, work, and hope together
Towards gaining brighter tomorrows
Succeeding in this sweet land of Liberty.
Give us Work, Purpose, Promise, and Equality.

John Graves Morris *is the author of* Noise and Stories *and also the manuscript of a second collection* The County Seat of Wanting So Many Things *that has been languishing so far unpublished, has recently had poems appear in* Volume One, Big Muddy, *and* The Concho River Review. *A veteran Woody poet and Professor of English at Cameron University, he lives in Lawton.*

Ode to a Kick-ass Framer

> *Once I built a railroad; I made*
> *it run, made it race*
> *against time.*
> *Once I built a railroad; now*
> *it's done. Brother, can*
> *you spare a dime?*
> E. Y. Harburgh

As a graduation gift, my father, who
was unemployed at the time, gave me his
father's well-worn copy of Rudyard
Kipling's poems, one of Grampa's most
prized possessions, which Dad remembered
his father reading as he sat with a beer on
the porch after work and from which he
frequently recited out loud, something Dad
had just inherited after his older
brother's death. Right before he drove
over for my ceremony, accompanied by a
friend to save on gas, Dad found a crumpled
piece of paper in the student union of his
hometown college on which an undergraduate
poet had begun to scrawl an ode to a "kick-
ass framer," a carpenter, most likely his
father. Accompanied on this trip by a
cooler of cheap beer to placate his sketchy
friend, who insisted on sleeping outside
our apartment on a chaise lounge,
mortifying my girlfriend, Dad spent a lot
of the weekend after the ceremony rereading

the rough poem and recalling my
grandfather. Grampa was, he said, a
skilled carpenter, and someone whom I had
never met because he had died three months
before my father's twentieth birthday--he
had been fifty when Dad was born—and about
whom Dad had seldom spoken before. Fueled
perhaps by leftover beer and possibly
reappraising him because he was now dealing
with unemployment at an advanced age
himself and associating with erratic ne'er-
do-wells like the lounge sleeper more than
he ever had before, Dad filled that weekend
with cutting and sawing and hammering and
nailing together the portrait of my
grandfather that has since hung in the
gallery of my imagination because the only
picture of him I have ever seen, and then
just once, was a small, out-of-focus
photograph taken by Dad's older sister.

To Dad, my grandfather had lived for
most of his life like Tom Sawyer, a life of
high spirits and adventures and probably
foolishness, though about that last I'm not
completely certain; I do know, however,
that at age twenty-five, he boldly left
home in Kentucky, abandoning his first
family, and moved to Oklahoma to help build
the railroad. From him, Dad had learned to
value and take care of his tools, the most
neatly arranged and cared-for things he
owned, to see and follow the grain in wood
whenever he cut or sanded, and not to let
water near, and thus rot, wooden utensils.
Walking around his hometown as a boy, Dad
told me he swelled with pride to see the
things his father had helped build.

56

Grampa, grown too old to play ball, would
encourage Dad to race while he looked on,
and Dad said that he would run like the
wind. Garrulous and engaging, Grampa was
quick to put on a pot of coffee whenever
anyone stopped by the house and settle in
for an evening of talk and laughter,
especially as he got older, no doubt
irritating my grandmother at times.

　　　Then he lost his job in the worst days
following the stock market crash of 1929,
was untrained for anything else and really
too old then to learn another job. I
wonder how my father regarded him at that
time, especially after my grandmother,
twenty years Grampa's junior and with a
child still in the house, Dad, divorced him
because he could not provide for his
family. Grampa ended up having to rely upon
friends, relatives, and the dole, dying in
a nursing home after surgery for prostate
cancer. At the end of his life, like so
many others then, he had become so much
scrap lumber to take to the dump. Dad, who
was still in Europe at the end of the
Second World War and could not get
permission to come home for the funeral,
never really forgave my grandmother even
though she, with an eighth-grade education,
had had to go work as a maid for horse
farmers to support the two of them, even
getting remarried to a well-to-do man she
didn't love before Dad left for the Army.
What stood out the clearest in Dad's
musings was that even though he had not
finished high school and did not have many
intellectual pursuits, Grampa loved poetry,

revered and delighted in reciting Kipling's thumpers out loud, getting caught up in the rhythmic lilt and rhyme, but also deeply respecting the written word, something that Dad came to share. I now frequently pull out the well-loved collection and reread Kipling's poems, trying to conjure the voice of that "better man than I," that kick-ass framer.

Julie Chappell *In her former life as a professor of medieval and early modern English literature and creative writing, Julie A. Chappell published six books of scholarship and a collection of her original poetry,* Faultlines: One Woman's Shifting Boundaries *(Village Books Press, 2013). Since retiring, she has had two more collections of poetry and two collections of short stories published:* Mad Habits of a Life *(Lamar University Literary Press, 2019),* As I Pirouette Away *(Turning Plow Press, 2021),* Homecoming and Other Mythic Tales *(Fine Dog Press, 2021), and* Contrary Qualities of Elements *(Fine Dog Press, 2023). She lives on Lake Keystone near Tulsa, Oklahoma with her poet husband, Hank Jones, and their four cats.*

Holiday Joys

The flashing and blinking single strand
is my neighbor's way of hanging onto
Christmas
with a vengeance.

Her tree, dry and fading inside the artificial air

looks more like a stalk of tinder
than an emblem of celebration.
As its lights flash on,

Fire! I think,

as I start from sleep—
her porch and tree blinking
while the lights from the
24-hour mart
highlight the night.

Burrowing further into my insufficient cocoon

where my toes stick out or my head gets cold
contemplating winter nights and Christmas lights,
my neighbor pulls in from her night shift job

turns off her blinking lights so she can sleep

'til night brings celebration on again.

At the QT

If I could,
I would draw her—
high cheekbones
strong jaw
swirl of midnight hair
against skin like
whipped chocolate
the fierceness in her eyes
as she clutches
her little girl tightly
close to her chest
the white bloated man
using his car
to push them
out of the way.

Badges for my father

Countless hours smiling, sharing
your love of human interaction
even the simplest kind with a new
badge for which you gave chits,
made change, offered directions.

But that badge left you in the margins
of a life you once lived, of service
to all, that badge had declared your worth.
The new badge proclaimed you just'
another squirrel frantically moving the wheel.

Child of a world that promised
opportunity for all, if you only—

worked hard, pursued your dreams—
rewards would come. But your dreams,
your rewards, faded long before you did.

Keely Record *lives in Tulsa, Oklahoma. She received an MFA from the Red Earth Creative Writing MFA program at Oklahoma City University and serves on the editorial board of* Nimrod International Journal. *Her poetry has appeared in* Atlas Poetica *and* Bamboo Hut.

Night Quiet

I step out of an imposed sanctuary
into night air icy
listen to silence
no leaf chatter
dead air

I escape warmth
to hear space void
of sound
but rev of cars street-race
against aloneness

I shock my senses
in the midnight sky
brittle cold
lone train rumbles
clatters breaks
the quiet

I find relief from four walls
engulfed by chilled darkness
stillness permeates
jake brake of a solitary
truck driver resonates
in the lull.

Harvest

Corn loses milky tenderness
yet not hard as feed
shuck and pull silk
from its rows
cut once shallow
cut again to the core
tote pot to roof, spread kernels
on rock-anchored sheets
dry under the sun

Among the corn
black-eyed peas grow
pods dry crackle
roll between hands
wind hauls hulls away
peas fall to galvanized tub
oven de-germinates for storage

More pink than orange
washed in a watery whiteness
dull hue of field pumpkins
peel and cube for long simmer
fills pie crusts
seeds rinsed, dried, jarred
keep the strain alive

Marigolds repel those that
destroy a harvester's bounty
each plant seeds a thousand selves
petals shed their orange and yellow
pluck grey-brown pods
drop in paper bag
to emerge in spring

Heels

Bare feet greened from mowing
walk newly tilled fields
push hand plow
to dispense seed
mound earth for squash
pick cantaloupe, tomatoes
before the chicken's peck

Skin torn in the soft arch
caught on barbed wire
cut tender okra
before the heat
before the fuzz imbeds itself
into your fingers

Feet stuck with spines
hoe weeds with petite
purple flowers
thorns hide under leaf
that leather in the sun
bite the sole

feet splayed
as watermelons crack
in ground collision
avoid pocket knife
that cuts the heart
warm and sweet
Sturdy heels made for hard work
or so I was told

Ken Hada *is the author of ten collections of poetry, including* Contour Feathers *(Turning Plow Press, 2021) winner of the Oklahoma Book Award. His work has been featured across the country in multiple venues, locations and occasions. His manuscript,* Come Before Winter, *will soon be released from Turning Plow Press.*

Janitor

His existence is a blues tune
that he wished could be played
in Memphis, where he visited
on his precious few days off
from cleaning the halls and bathroom
stalls with mop and bucket, his
quiet demeanor masking tunes
only he knows, private riffs,
wrong turns way back when, muddy times
recalled in sweeping rhythms
late at night on a lonely stage.

We Have These Witnesses

These men
These gnarly men
With twisted frames
Sun-slant eyes
Grizzled hair

These men
Squatting heel to heel
In a wheat field at sundown
Remembering tomorrow's burden

These men
Witness to my future

Witness to a land
That vows to break them
To wind that won't let them be

These women
Who bore hope
With quilting hands
Hammered forearms
That look good still
In a Sunday-red dress
With a pink rose

These women
Who notice the flycatcher in flight
Who snap garden beans
And wring necks of fryers
Plow October ground
In alternating furrows
Of hope and doom –
Hope and the alternative
Too dark to consider
Too bleak to imagine

These witnesses
Immigrants
Stalking freedom like predators
Building community
Like fire ants in usurped soil
Living beyond the fenced lines
Of failure and success
Determined by work
Wedded to a new land
Haunted by the "Old Country"

Return like sunflowers
Gritty and God-fearing

The Working Poor

They gather before sunrise
at a convenience store – a neon
oasis where a cowboy-hatted
man reads the morning paper

We hold these truths to be
self-evident ...

The clerk sports a turquoise
muscle shirt & camo cap – his pale, red
flesh matches his eyes – gas, coffee,
sodas, bad breakfast,
ATM money for a bus ticket

We are all starting over,
aren't we?

Kim Gentry Meyer *As editor of both her high school and college newspapers, Kim has always loved composing and editing the written word. For over twenty-two years she's continued to hone these skills as a professional grant writer, raising over $20 million for nonprofit causes. She especially enjoys coaching others on how to make their own writing more persuasive using her three guiding principles: Keep It Simple, Stay Positive, and Use What You Already Know. Kim is no stranger to WoodyFest, having won 2nd place in the 2013 Woody Guthrie Folk Festival Songwriting Contest for her original song, "How I Wanna Be."*

You'll Find Me There

When your prayers are more than habit
And my verses more than lines
When communion's more than kneeling
To take the bread and wine
You'll find me there

When there's peace instead of slander
And you seek to understand
When you care for all creation
When you lend a helping hand
You'll find me there

When the weight is on your shoulders
And the poor become your own
When you choose to love the haters
And you take the higher road
You'll find me there

When your treasures bless my Kingdom
Instead of earthly gain
When your joy is found in serving
And you give instead of take
You'll find me there

A Tree's Just a Tree

Thirty years he stood

On a concrete floor
And I know there are times
That he wanted more
Than that slaughterhouse job
And that secondhand car
But he was doin' the best he could

She wrapped her world around her kids

And we all wondered what might have been

If her mama had lived
And someone had given
A damn about who she could be

If I could go back

I'd shake that family tree
If I could go back
I'd rewrite history
So many things I would change
If I could go back

But I can't go back

So I'll walk straight ahead
Mama and Daddy please know that you've led
Me to a better life
Than you were able to find

And though history has a way
Of coming back around
This time I'm ready

and I'll stand my ground
The future's up to me
Because roots are just roots

And a tree's just a tree.

Ky George *Inspired equally by her upbringing on the plains of Oklahoma and time spent exploring the high desert of New Mexico, Ky George uses essay, fiction, and poetry to explore the intimate relationships between the land and its people. Ky is a graduate of the Red Earth MFA and has had work published in* The Oklahoma Review, Insurrection, *and* Lesbians are Miracles.

If There is a God

If there is a god, I believe she is the girl working the
register at the fried-pie-stand-slash-gas station, her voice
an
unmistakable Okie twang promising to go after the two
men who just shorted them on their $20 order. Instead of
flowing robes, she wears a worn red visor, faded acne
scars marking her sacred cheeks, bands of keloid grease
burns adorning her wrists.

If there is a god, I believe she's the barista on the
weekday opening shift who infers, after my third 6 AM
visit in a
week, that I'm a teacher, and asks how the kids are doing
at
a school she's never heard of. Instead of a gleaming
crown,
she wears her golden hair in silken braids, barely-
tarnished silver rings weighing on her fingers.

If there is a god, I believe he is the analyst who, a lifetime
before occupying a claustrophobic cubicle, hopped a
midnight train and rode until he found an apple orchard a
half a country away from home. Instead of a blessed
stole,

he wears a polished-turquoise bolo tie, rusted spurs
clasped along his heels.

If there is a god, I believe they are the medium in the
small hippie town with the roadside bar, who tells
fortunes to travelers and once promised me that frogs
would be an important force on the journey ahead.
Instead of relics,
they carry a worn set of tarot cards, silken scarves knotted
carefully around their neck.

If there is a god, I believe she is the drunk woman in the
bar who says "Merry Christmas" like a threat.

If there is a god, I believe he is the boy who put the
groceries from the food bank in his backpack before the
others could see.

If there is a god, I believe she is the waitress with the
shaved head who always remembers the oat milk for my
coffee.

If there is a god, I wonder if they could possibly compare
to the least of these.

Linda Neal Reising *a native of Oklahoma and citizen of the Western Cherokee Nation, has been published in numerous journals, including* The Southern Indiana Review, The Comstock Review, *and* Nimrod. *She was named the winner of the 2012 Writer's Digest Poetry Competition, and her work has been nominated for a Pushcart Prize three times. Her chapbook,* Re-Writing Family History *(Finishing Line Press), was a finalist for the 2015 Oklahoma Book Award, as well as winner of the 2015 Oklahoma Writers' Federation Poetry Book Prize. The Keeping (Finishing Line Press), her first full-length book of poetry, won the 2020 Kops-Fetherling Phoenix Award for Outstanding New Voice in Poetry. Her second full-length book,* Stone Roses *(Kelsay Books), was a finalist for the 2022 WILLA Award and the Oklahoma Book Award, as well as winning the Eric Hoffer Award and the Western Heritage Wrangler Award.*

Made in America

My father was one of the men who,
coming back, shed his Army uniform,
traded his sniper rifle for textbooks,
meaning to milk the G.I. bill for a monthly
check as he sat in junior college classes,
surrounded by teenage girls drawing hearts
across their notebooks, writing Elvis, Marlon,
or Tab inside. He did not mean to fall in love
with learning, which only made the break-up
of graduation harder, when he had to face
his fate—a man with a family needed the factory
pay. For thirty years he donned his navy blue
pocket tees and crepe-soled shoes, carried his lunch
bucket, shaped like a black metal barn. He chewed
Beechnut as he lifted, pulled, cut—creating tires
on an assembly line. In summer, when temperatures
blazed, he popped salt tablets that turned his sweat
white. And every few years, he walked the picket
lines during strikes to demand a quarter raise.
Stench of rubber resided inside his nose, and he

did not know as he dipped his fingers into benzene
or wiped carbon black away with his hanky
that he was holding his own death in his hands,
as he numbed his mind, toiled away, night
after night on the graveyard shift.

The Hands She Was Dealt

My mother thought she had been dealt
the king of hearts when my father, wearing
his pleated Carey Grant pants and glossy
black boots sauntered into Woolworth's,
scoped out the merchandise, and headed
toward the candy counter, moat of glass,
enclosing heaped red hots and chocolate
kisses. Ruby, his cousin who worked
the sock department, keeping the pairs
matched and folded, had arranged
for him to purchase a pack of Juicy Fruit,
and if he liked my mother's smile, red
lips blooming with Helena Rubinstein's
Bed of Roses, he was to introduce himself,
suggest a Coke at the lunch counter. Mother's
hands, nails trimmed and unpolished—dime
store regulation—must have shaken, counting
back his change. And when she took his hand
eleven months later, she thought her farmgirl
days, left behind after high school graduation,
were a dusty memory, traded for Loretta
Young dresses and fancy Jell-O molds, not
knowing his dream was to leave the town,
own a few acres, her life thrown in reverse

For thirty years, she dropped seeds into holes,
turned potato eyes down, picked beans and peas,
flicked worms from tomato leaves, gathered

clutches of warm eggs from nests, twisted
chickens' necks when they were too old
to lay, pinched their singed pin feathers,
her fingers plucking them like mournful
harp strings.

The Head of the Union Escorts Frances Perkins, U.S. Secretary of Labor, through the Mines—1940

Welcome to the Ozark foothills, filled with galena
and jack. Step into the can and hold on, the mines
are deep and dark. Here is where armies of Okies
and Missouri plowboys did their part in the War to
End All Wars that didn't, digging the lead
for bullets and shot. Come hear about the camps—
Cardin, Century, Picher—all towns now, not nearly
as many brawls and knives driven through ribs.
Still, young men are dying. Note the pillars
of rock, some fifty feet thick, left in place, creating
space for the shovelers, boys just old enough to
grow a shadow of manhood. Watch
as they brim each bucket, biceps bulging,
as they race to fill sixty or seventy a day—a weight
of thirty, forty tons or more—getting paid a nickel
for each. No, they don't last long before moving
on to become machine men, if the liquor
that gets them through doesn't get them first.
Young men are dying. They fall to falling roofs
and explosions set too soon. And there is always
the dust, made of flinty chert with splinters,
tiny daggers, stabbing their lungs. Please
don't make promises you can't keep. The miners
have trouble a plenty, but they also know false

hopes when they see them. Fooled too often,
they don't let themselves in for another deception.
They know what life has to offer them—
a two-room rented shack and a prayer for cash
to buy a radio. But they still work until they can't
anymore, leave families to the mercy of charities.
Just remember, Mrs. Perkins, young men are dying.

Some of the words in this poem were taken from a speech by Tony McTeer, former miner and district CIO president.

Molly Sizer *is a retired rural sociologist living in southwest Oklahoma. Her research focused on socio-economic inequalities, mostly at work and in rural areas. She now spends her time walking and picking up trash in the Wichita Mountains, and occasionally writing poetry. She's presented poems at Lawton's Third Saturday readings, Duncan's Reading Down the Plains, the 2018 and 2022 Woody Poets readings, and the 2019 and 2022 Scissortail Festivals. Her work has been published in* Westview *and* The Oklahoma Review.

Hard Luck

Some white working men don't understand
why they're dealt such a losing hand.
Affirmative Action never won them a promotion.
They can't play the race, or the gender cards;
and they'll be damned if they take a trick
from the non-gendered suits.

They didn't draw a wealth card either. Investing
rules keep changing; antes keep rising.
Credit cards stay out of balance.
Taxes and insurance eat away
at earnings. They can't plan
on any inheritance from their parents.

And still they don't understand why the decks
are stacked against them.
They finished school, went to church and
got married; they bought a home
and a mortgage, and raised
their children to be good Christians.

Their trump cards are failing fast
as the far-left, fat-cats buy
big-city votes with other people's money.
Jokers in the public schools brain-
wash and bluff their children with scams

like critical race and global climates.

They're forced to draw a healthcare
card, costing more than the price
of uncovered prescription
drugs and dentists.
Meanwhile, the Medicaid mooches
pay practically nothing.

But at the rallies, faces painted with patriotic
colors, when it's finally their turn
to deal, no one cares if their nails
are cracked and packed
with grease and dirt. Their God promised
them a better hand in heaven.

Again

I wonder whether
I'm obligated,
as an amateur
photographer,

to watch another

beating video
from the body
cameras of officers
of the peace;

to observe the

unspeakable
actions of police
up close, from
their own point of view.

Should I allow
this additional evil
to burn my corneas
and etch new neural
pathways to fear?

I already know

what evil looks like:
Jesus on the cross
with nails in his feet
so he can never
        walk again.

Nathan Brown *is an author, singer-songwriter, and award-winning poet living in Wimberley, Texas. He served as Poet Laureate of Oklahoma in 2013-14. He's published over 25 books of poetry and memoir. His most recent collection of poems is* In the Days of Our Resilience, *the fourth in a series now known as the* Pandemic Poems Project, *that deals with the year of the pandemic. And his new travel memoir* Just Another Honeymoon in France: A Vagabond at Large, *is a prose romp through Paris and the Bordeaux region. An earlier book,* Two Tables Over, *won the Oklahoma Book Award.*

Full Of Hope

It's a beautiful
Sunday afternoon
out here on the back
county roads with no
shoulders, to speak of,
in the Texas Hill Country.

And so, since the preacher
at the First Baptist Church
finally wrapped up his
brimstone laced with
fire an hour or so ago,
there's now the popopop
of hot automatic gunfire
a few properties over.
Boys gotta have
something to do
while the roast
is in the oven.

They wanna kill
somebody. Though,
they may never...
it is possible...
get around to it.

Or, we could say,
have the privilege.
But they can hope,
can't they? Right?

Hope's a good thing.

You're Not Alone

If you're only beginning to feel it...
if any of this is about to make
sense to you for the first
time... you're okay.
It's not your fault.

The world is a blur.
Everyone else appears
to be moving much faster.
Your smartphone model is slated
for obsoletion soon. They don't even
manufacture that kind of battery anymore.
With every new operating system update,
you no longer know how to use a device.
You are not on TikTok... as we speak...
and Twitter, from inception, was an insult
to your expensive, long-endured education.

You don't want anything as fast as
Amazon delivers it. You do not
enjoy shopping, and all you did
was click on that little heart...
to turn it red... on Carmax.com,
and now they're texting and calling,
and that's causing you palpitations...
so you're just thinking about giving up
driving altogether, dear God in heaven.

But, you don't—because you live about
ten miles out of town now. So you can't.
It is where you moved to be tucked in
way behind a ranch gate at the far end
of a cul-de-sac because, that way, you
will never have anything resembling
through-traffic... not ever again...

Hail Mary, the Mother of Jesus.
Because, like Bukowski, you
don't hate people... you "just
feel better when they're not around."
Much like you don't hate Starbucks...
you just cannot comprehend a hundred
and twenty-five different ways to say coffee.

So maybe you grocery shop at night? Right?
So there won't be anyone shoving samples
of corn chips and hot salsa in your face—
and the self-checkout'll always be open.
And you go to the small, local stores,
because the starship Whole Foods
has too many weird French cheeses
to choose from, as well as too many
forms of finely-sliced Italian bacon,
or ham, or whatever the hell that stuff
is, with all those unpronounceable names.

And maybe you're feeling fairly worn out
by this poem, because there is only
so much self-recognition one
can handle in one sitting.

So just know you're okay.
And, it is not your fault...
that you're considering moving
to somewhere between the tundra

of the Torngat Mountains and the sandy
plateau of Happy Valley-Goose Bay
up in Newfoundland and Labrador.

This Quaking Earth

~ for Mesut Hancer, and his
daughter Irmak Kahramanmaras Turkey

The worst of the quake's aftershocks
shook your soul down to a deeper
level of the hell surrounding you.
All that was left for the eyes to see
were the pale fingers of a soft hand
on the dirty corner of her mattress.

Her blanket draped and drooping
to the rubble below... one giant
pink tear falling on broken tile.
A flag lowered after the battle.
A loss in the war of all fathers.
At least those who dared to love.

And whether this was a seismic
god, an angry earth—or some
act of geological indifference—
what does that matter to you now
and forever forward... as you sit
in the ruins of Kahramanmaras

with nothing left for a father to do
but stay put, lean forward in frozen
air, reach out... and hold the pale
fingers of that soft hand, as long
as it will take for them to come and
free the rest of what does not remain?

Paul Austin's *most recent book is* Spontaneous Behavior, the Art and Craft of Acting, *published by Turning Plow Press in 2022, His poetry collection,* Notes on Hard Times, *was published by Village Books Press. His work has appeared in* This Land, Sugar Mule, Oklahoma Review, More Monologues by Men, *and* Newport Review. *His poems have also been included in* Speak Your Mind, *the 2019 anthology of* Woody Guthrie Poets, *and* Bull Buffalo and Indian Paintbrush, *an anthology of Oklahoma poetry,* Behind the mask: Haiku in the Time of Covid-19, Jerry Jazz Musician, *and* LEVEL Land: poems for and about the I-35 corridor. Late Night Conspiracies, *a collection of his writings, was performed with jazz ensemble at New York's Ensemble Studio Theatre. More about his writing and his life in the theatre can be found on his website:* https://paustin.net.

The Ferry

She came from Nova Scotian men,
who pick by pick, dug out company coal till one by
one they wore out limbs and lungs.

The women fed, cleaned, consoled,
prayed the Virgin for the strength to endure.

The poverty surrounding her,
its gnawing hunger and its progression
of untimely deaths had blurred her senses.

An unconscious apprehension
of anonymity had numbed her mind.

It was difficult to remain
loyal to the life assigned, her prayers
for help were but recitations.

She declined all consolation,
afraid to pacify her hope for change.

She yearned to answer the demand of
her young, restless body, impatient for a
life she could call her own.

Shrouded in morning fog, she boarded
a ferry from Halifax to Boston toward
an unknown future ahead...

For Michael Moody

playwright, poet, seaman
and maker of things

We all arrive wounded at birth
and those who pretend otherwise
presume their cruel authority
as right to abuse and control.

But here's a man who won't submit,
who carries the scars of old wounds
like birthmarks; badges of honor
to quell the fear, claim his selfhood,

get on with the work of living,
labor to make those useful things
from eye and mind, muscle and heart
that leave behind what matters most:

a legacy of work well done,
a lexis of courage and hope
for those he loves and who love him
and all of us born to the wound.

Two Actors Work Overtime

in Charlie's Bar two a.m.

1: It's geological…
    the whole damn thing…
    geological…

2: Mmm…

1. Layers…it's all layers…

2. Mmm…

1: acting… Is geological…

2: Oh… okay…

Silence. They drink.

1: No… wait a sec…
    not quite right…

2. Oh….?

1: Think about it…

2: Okay…

1: Acting….

    is *archeological*…
    character… is *geological*…

2. Ah… okay… yeah…

1. That's the work, see… ?
    dig down…layers…
    recover the past…

2: Yeah... past... in present...
   makes a character...

1: Bingo!

The bartender smiles; it's closing time.

Paul Juhasz *was born in western New Jersey, grew up just outside New Haven, Connecticut, and has spent appreciable chunks of his life in the plains of central Illinois, in the upper hill country of Texas, and in the Lehigh Valley in Pennsylvania. Most recently seduced by the spirit of the red earth, he now lives in Oklahoma City. A graduate of the Red Earth M.F.A., his work has appeared in several literary journals, most recently* Concho River Review, Poetry Quarterly, Oklahoma Review *and* Main Street Rag. *He has been serving as curator and coordinator of the* Woody Guthrie Poets *since 2020.* His first book, Fulfillment: Diary of a Warehouse Picker—*a mock journal covering his six-month stint in an Amazon warehouse—was published by Fine Dog Press in 2020. His second book,* Ronin, *a collection of (mostly) prose poems—also published by Fine Dog Press—was named a finalist for the 2022 Oklahoma Book Award in poetry. His second collection of poetry,* The Inner Life of Comics, *was published by Turning Plow Press in the fall of 2022.*

Baggage

On this cool, wind-scoured final day of the year, I watch a figure and his suitcase gimp across the faded-fawn park grass. It's over 60 degrees, but he's huddled against the uncertainty of future weather. Faded down jacket the color of static, what was once a tattered scarf around the neck, the insistent defiance of a cowboy hat.

Later tonight, better-dressed crowds will gather in warm rooms, with their hors d'oeurvres and champaign and the paper-thin security of trinkets, blithely unaware of the suffocating weight of their collective errata.

This lurching man, prophet and prophecy, will not be among them. Nor his suitcase, not dragged like he's a misplaced traveler, but clutched to his chest like a prized possession or a beloved child.

I do not know if this is a relocation or a disburdening, but understand either is more instructive than the counting down of minutes and seconds, or the hollow celebration of false renewal and soon-to-be-broken resolutions.

A Fragmented Mythology

"Til human voices wake us / and we drown"
T.S. Eliot

1.

They are the labyrinth and the Minotaur both. But that has never been enough. So they look to the heavens with envy, and they build wings, and leave us to breathe in the miasma they leave behind.

2.

As I drive across the nearly-hundred-year-old bridge, the workers look like insects, scurrying about the spine of the new bridge that will replace it. They showed up to work today in Fords and Chevys, with sandwiches of tuna or egg salad on white bread caried in metal pails or re-used plastic bags from Wal-Mart. Some will have thermoses of coffee, others will make do with water. If their collars were ever blue, they've long since becomes grime and sweat-stained.

3.

Hercules pulled a fast one on Atlas. Tricked him into covering his shift. Hercules went on to fame, his legend known for millennia, had The Rock (oh, the irony of it being The Rock) play him in a movie. Atlas was left to bear the weight. Hercules didn't understand all the profits went to Zeus anyway.

4.

There is a natural history museum in Pittsburgh. To
prepare specimens for exhibit, they use the larvae of a
species of beetle to strip flesh from bone. The cleaned
bone is then assembled and displayed. This museum, like
most things in Pittsburgh, bears Andrew Carnegie's name.
As if the things within, the bones and meteorites and
assorted artifacts, were his.

5.

There are new gods among us. They are self-proclaimed.
They think the story of King Midas is porn. They project
themselves into the stratosphere to look down upon us.
We must look like insects from there. Boxer telling
Napoleon, "I will work harder"—our new national
anthem—delightful music to these news gods, like
prayers to old Olympus.

6.

When the bridge is finished, it will bear a new god's
name, but it will not be his bridge. It has never been his
bridge. It belongs to the workers who, when rheumatic
and torn by labor and bills, will still be able to shuffle
weary and broken feet to the edge of the river's bank,
point at the steel spine spanning its width, turn to wide-
eyed grandchildren and say, "I built this,"

And somewhere, off in the corner of this tableau, a
splash, something will plummet into the cold dark depths
of the swirling river.

And that will be Icarus.

Regina Philpott McLemore *Like many Oklahoma Cherokees, Regina McLemore's 's ancestors walked the Trail of Tears. Her historical series, Cherokee Passages, relates stories they might have told about the Trail and their lives in Indian Territory. Her work has appeared in several publications, and she is a columnist for* Saddlebag Dispatches. *Her first historical novel,* Cherokee Clay, *which received a Will Rogers medallion, was published in 2020.* Cherokee Stone *was released in 2021, followed by* Cherokee Steel *in 2022. McLemore lives in rural Oklahoma with her husband Dennis and their cats and dog. When she's not writing, she enjoys visiting family, writing, reading, volunteering, traveling, and working in her flowers.*

Tale of a Working Man

Like Woody, and a lot of Okies, once upon a time, my
father lived in the Land of Dreams.
A place where a working man had a chance to make
some "real" money,
A place where it never snowed, and the soil stayed put,
A place where a working man might overcome the hard
hand he had been dealt.

California called his name with its prosperity promises,
As it had called Woody, Dad's uncles, and close cousins
years before.
So, like a poor peddler, he put all he could carry in a
single suitcase,
Bought a train ticket and steadfastly made his way
westward.

California kin with little to share would share what little
they had,
Until such time as he could maintain his own slim
subsistence.
He picked produce, drove trucks, and did whatever
work he could find,
And soon agreed with Woody that "A workin' man's

hand is the hardest card in the whole damn deck to
play."

Finally, he discovered decent labor unions that protected
their workers' rights.
As he attended many meetings, and like a school boy,
learned lessons,
That would enlighten, enlarge, and elevate his view of
the world,
To actively advocate for politicians who honestly
support the blue-collar worker.

Although similar in his thinking, at heart, he wasn't a
wandering Woody.
Even though he adapted and advanced, one day he
answered a spirit call,
Which caught and hauled him back home like a fish on
a line,
Still fighting to win with the working man's cards he
had been dealt.

Richard Dixon *is a retired high-school Special Education teacher and tennis coach. He has had his poetry, fiction and non-fiction published in* Dragon Poet Review, Conclave, Crosstimbers, Westview, Red Earth Review, Red River Review, Red Earth Forum, Oklahoma Today, Walt's Corner of the Long Islander, HARD CRACKERS, *3 Woody Guthrie anthologies in 2011, 2013 and 2017 as well as* Clash By Night, *an anthology of poems related to the breakthrough 1979 album by the Clash,* London Calling. *He has been a featured reader at Full Circle Bookstore, the Depot in Norman, OK, the Benedict St. Marketplace and Lunch Box in Shawnee, OK, the Scissortail Creative Writing Festival in Ada, OK, the Chikaskia Literary Festival in Tonkawa, OK. and the annual Woody Guthrie readings in Oklahoma City, Okemah and Tulsa, OK. He is the author of a chapbook of poems,* Leaving Home *(2017).*

A Workin' Man's Hand Is The Hardest Card In The Whole Damn Deck To Play

The one summer after the second year of teaching
was one of my busiest, driving a supply truck
for a large roofing company from 6 to 4
then cleaning up, early dinner and umpire baseball
till 10 p.m.

Felt good to be thus occupied and making money
for my wife and 2-child family, felt worthwhile
until I discovered my wife in bed with my best friend
Then the whole damn thing changed, and I got an
attitude.

I got your bossa-nova la-roca, got your Lee Iacocca
sit up straight on your horse
you Randolph Scott-lookin' motherfucker.

Actually, you're L.Q. Jones, Cowboy #2

don't movie-set me, my role only grew
you sat on that but the fuse till blew.

Hit me in the face, ain't nothin' but a six-pack
your life another day in a kickback
back to where it always belonged.

Any message from me bound to be
at least 3-pronged, always righted, never wronged
outskirted or saronged.

Workin' man my whole life, the weight to carry me
Randolph Scott, into the next century, mile by mile
I squinted, cowboy-style.

Workin' man's hand sometimes hard to ascertain
in any language, other than plainspoken and hard-barked
and any of the baser emotions sparked

down to a coarser grain, where even a splinter
don't bring no pain.

Rilla Askew *is the author of five novels, a book of stories, and collection of creative nonfiction. She's a PEN/Faulkner finalist and recipient of the Arts and Letters Award from the American Academy of Arts and Letters. Her novel about the 1921 Tulsa Race Massacre,* Fire in Beulah, *received the American Book Award in 2002. Askew's essays, poems, and short fiction have appeared in* AGNI, Tin House, World Literature Today, Nimrod, TriQuarterly, *and elsewhere. She teaches at the University of Oklahoma.*

Shadow Work Force

Inside the plant, the oven blasts, the dough
is thick, Juanito's arms are pink and hairless
as a baby's. He shoves the heavy tray of chip-
flecked dough inside the gaping, blackened maw,
but pulls back quick. Last week he bent too close,
the burdened tray an afterthought, his mind on
Rosalita. He has no eyebrows now. His sponsor
says, Forget it, man, they'll grow again.

This is his night job, to bake the Quaker Chewy
bars, the crunchy oat granola ones for Nature Valley.
By day he skates down slanted roofs, his shoulders
bowed by drooping packs of heavy asphalt shingles.
He's safer now, he tells himself, with his new shoes.
The sponsor charged him for the shoes, another cost
he writes in Spanish inside his spiral notebook pages:

ropas: Walmart clothes—tee-shirts, jeans.
tacos—eaten in the sponsor's truck
the day he took him shopping.
zapatillos deportiva—his running shoes,
good rubber soles that cling to plank and wood
so he won't die like Carlos did: a trip, a slip,
a silent fall. A crooked x upon the ground.
The men along the rooftop shouting.

Inside the plant, the oven roars its ruthless heat,
the breath of *el diablo*. Again, again, for hours
on end, he feeds the trays of khaki dough into
the devil's maw, his mind on Rosalita. He dreams
her as she works: her small hands quick to stuff
sealed bags of little Os inside the cheerful yellow
boxes. Cheerios, the label says. He sees her
worried frown, her netted hair pulled tight.

Last week she saw her cousin's hair get caught
beneath a metal claw, a bloody wedge of scalp
ripped off. Rosalita works the midnight shift, like him;
they meet outside before their shifts, filing in with
others in the dark: shy looks, big smiles, a quick
exchange of longing. She goes to school by day,
so when she falls asleep in class is not so *peligroso*.
as when Juanito tires and nods and drifts to sleep
perched on his heels at peak of roof inside a chimney's
shadow. His dreams are kind. His boss is not. His boss
will shout and curse and sometimes hit the boys: José,
Ramon, Luis, Enrique. Not Carlos now, the youngest
one. His broken body in a box. Shipped home for smaller
cost than his family paid to bring him here. Juanito
wakens with a start. The oven roars. The chewy bars are
burnt. They'll dock his pay. He quickly loads another tray.

He shoves it in the devil's mouth, his heart despairing.
His mind's eye sees the scribbled page: his name,
the list, the costs for shoes, clothes, haircut, toothbrush,
papers filed, his work permit, his fake ID, and at the top:
primer pago salido Guatemala a los Estados Unidos:
10,000 *quetzales*, the biggest cost, the one Juanito alone
must pay. He tries and tries to pay, he hardly eats, he
never sleeps, but every day the purchase list grows longer.

Midway on the Turner Turnpike

after Returning the Gift
7.17.92

I want to love you better,
you fathers who are my father,
you white men in Oklahoma.
I want to love you men with
sunburned faces, hair gone white
or silver, thinning over foreheads
spotted, you men with cowboy
in your face, and farmer, rancher,
eyes slitted in the sunlight
as you stand in line now at
McDonald's, wrong somehow
in this vinyl place: shoulders
humped beneath plaid and piping,
your voice in drawl and splinter
asking for your senior citizen's
discount meal.

Tomorrow, or the next day,
I will love you, when your arm
reaches from the turnpike window,
your sunburned freckled arm
so like my father's, as you
take my toll and offer me good
wishes for my day: your blue
eyes dim in shade and shadow,
crinkled from a sun long
since set.

Tomorrow, or the next day,
I won't remember the smashed
turtle's shell beaten open with
a hammer because that turtle
ate your catfish eggs. I won't

remember the barn owl caught
in your smart trap, one taught
you by a cousin or an uncle,
a neighbor, some other white
man who knew how to catch
a barn owl by the claw and
teach it one good lesson:
never to eat your penned-up
laying hens, your mother guineas,
the working, pampered fowl
you've tamed.

Robin Wheeler *grew up in rural Missouri, and is a writer based in the St. Louis area. As a food and music journalist her work appeared in* The Riverfront Times, St. Louis Magazine, Sauce, Eleven, KDHX.com, *and* Monterey County Times. *Her essays have been in* The St. Louis Anthology *and* Knives and Ink. *She's a former Woody Guthrie Archives researcher, and has participated in Woody Guthrie Poets since 2018.*

Viv Made the Dungarees

Mick's fat-kneed factory girl
had no money, wore curlers in her hair,
and a taste for liquor in her stained dress and scarves.
Her man waited for her in the rain.

My factory girl tied a gossamer KMart scarf
over her tower of russet curls.
Red, like the old spilled blood of the
lamb who kept the liquor from her
throat.

Viv's man didn't wait outside.
He drove far-off byways.
Eighteen wheels and a union card
while she sewed the dungarees in the factory.

and raised their babies to hot rod years,
lowered their parents through twilight
in a saltbox house, linoleum and shag,
and an indoor toilet installed after Kennedy died.
Viv built the shelves, butchered the chickens,
sang the hymns, killed the snakes,
made her brother's deathbed
when a drunk's punch called him home.

She teased her hair with Dippity-Do,
sewed silky red dresses for church,

hugging the hips he loved.
Six days on the road and he's gonna make it home
tonight.

Cat-eye glasses and costume pearls,
low-heeled shoes with the straps on top,
and fleshy, crooked fingers gnarled
from days of denim and needles in her hands.

Pete the Wheeler

A divorcee of 23 and a Teamster milk truck
driver, drag raced a souped-up GTO
through the prairie night and
birthed me into a Springsteen song.

Pete Wheeler made wheels when the dairy closed.
Daytime sleeping, sunshine shunted.
Turn that music off and swat the dog
if she forgets and barks at the mailman.

Pete's pale steel eyes burned
from an Al Jolson face. His face, body covered in oil
like he hugged each wheel
to make the aluminum shine.
I would never work that hard.
Teen feet on concrete fourteen hours a day. But I
sucked up the money: clothes, records, roof. I was
soft as spoiled fruit.

Staying awake through nights,
boombox in my lap, Bruce in my ears,
singing about factories and my dad.
It all made sense in "Atlantic City,"
Not when he grabbed my shoulders and shook,
slapped the barrette from my hair,

promised to give me something to cry about.
As if I didn't have enough.

Mandatory overtime and perfect attendance awards
until rage stopped his heart on the line. Four
bypassed arteries and forced retirement with a
decade left unworked.

Now Pete limps to the barn
where he sells horse tack and guns.
A bag of bones and titanium, wondering
when the wheels came off.

Good Time Charlie's Last Ride

Charlie spent trucking money
on fancy cowboy boots. Tony Lamas and Freys
he displayed on the living room staircase,
polished and scuffless.

He'd tell me to fill my fists with quarters
overflowing his truck's ashtray
while he watched "Hee-Haw" and Tom T.
Hall, stone-faced through heartbreak songs.

A deep chuckle, a shamed head-shake,
"Mm-hmmmm" he replied to
"I love you."
"I miss you."

So cool he drove 18 wheels
six million miles without a wreck.
His only jack knife
Stashed in his front pocket.

They called him Good Time Charlie on the CB,
maybe for his temperance, his Pentecostal core,
or for reasons
granddaughters shouldn't know.
He told stories of robberies, dead bodies,
girls earning tuition at the rest stop, how he
loved the way Chicago opened wide at the
curve on 55.

He took his leave
below a painting of Jesus
guiding a trucker through the
storm, display case of awards at his
side,

A trucker pulled to the side of the road when
pumping fists emerged from the hearse,
sending Good Time Charlie home
with an airhorn howl announcing his arrival.

Ron Wallace *is an Oklahoma native from Durant, where he was born and raised. He is the author of ten books of poetry. Five have been finalists in the Oklahoma Book Awards with* Renegade and Other Poems *winning in 2018. His debut novel was also a finalist in fiction for 2021 Book Awards.*

The Way of the Buffalo

Too much of Oklahoma
has gone the way of the buffalo,
      just disappeared
into ink-stained pages on paper,
forgotten like rodeos of long ago.

Claremore clings to Will Rogers,
      like lost lovers
hold on to hope,
and Okemah's reclaimed
Woody Guthrie's ghost
      James Garner's
turned ten foot tall and solid bronze
to stand in the heart of Norman.

But Quanah Parker's here no more.
He went away by halves
      first the red half then the white.
Black Kettle bled out
      on Sand Creek banks
under his own American flag.
Ralph Ellison is almost invisible now,
and Jim Thorpe,
      lies buried
way up north
far away from plains and prairies
      Too many are gone,
buried like the bones of bison

beneath the native grass
or made into painted skulls
to hang on walls.

Complicit

I am the son of a cop
        a good man
who taught me to look past the badge
and beyond the uniform
        to see the human heart
that beats inside all of us.
I was brought to understand that
Justice denied leads to a nation laid to waste,
and I must not be complicit.
But now, I walk among bastards
who play by the same rules that govern piranhas
        men who lead
with the same ego as Custer
riding ahead of the Seventh Cavalry.
But these men will not fall with those they lead.
        These men
would burn Greenwood to the ground again
and go to church that next Sunday
believing God was on their side.
They lack compassion
courage
remorse,
but not stockpiles of ammunition.
Given the opportunity,
these men would devour the world
        swallow it whole
                and spit out the bones.

Just a Cowboy

Way down yonder in the Indian nation
a cowboy's life is my occupation.
~ Woody Guthrie

He's out there somewhere right now –
just a cowboy.
He's from Chugwater, Wyoming
      Broken Bow, Oklahoma
           Redcrest, California
riding rough stock in a rodeo for pocket change.

And every time Chris Ledoux sings
"One Ride in Vegas"
      he knows it's about him.
But bareback broncs ain't got no pity,
and I never saw a Brahma bull
that liked a cowboy
      sitting on his back.
No, it only takes eight seconds
      for ten years to spin away
out of a bucking chute like a West Texas tornado
leaving a grown man's youth bitin' dust.

Arkansas to Montana, Nevada to New Mexico
      he's just a cowboy
with a beat-up pickup truck,
cheap beer
      and busted bones.
And when the last go round is over,
it's all been said and done
      he'll most likely wind up alone,
what little money that he ever made, long gone
just a couple of friends
  to scatter the ashes
      and move on.

Sharon Frye *is a poet living in Northern Oklahoma. After 35 years of delivering mail for the USPS, she has retired. She enjoys rural photography as well as writing. Her chapbook,* Last Chance for Rain *was published in 2014 by Writing Knights Press. Her latest volume of poetry,* Blue Lamentations and Other Noisy Scrawls *was published by Cold River Press in March, 2017. Sharon has been invited to read her work in Ireland, Sacramento, Little Rock, Tulsa, Dallas and Oklahoma City. She has also featured in the symphony hall of her hometown of Enid, Oklahoma. Frye has also been published in numerous publications in the US, Ireland and Brazil.*

Detasseled

Under belched clouds in Nebraska's
sunny sky, irrigation pumps chugged
staccato rhythm, the zombie cadence
for marching pubescent pluckers.

She walked through miles of corn
heat swollen, wiry-haired stalks.
No breeze ruffled green leaves,
tousled yellow-silk tassels.

Budding songs played in her ears,
She yanked sticky plumes
with sweaty palms, pollen
rained over her freckled face.

August evaporated, as hot-
house mist in the summer sun.
It wasn't her plan to become
part of monster Monsanto

or lose her virginity in a cornfield.
She was earning money for college.

Morning Routine

She blindly reached for her coffee,
spilled it across his sports page.
Muddy stream dribbled on his khakis.
She heard twig-snap, small limbs
fell twisted. She thought of Oklahoma
storms, scream-pitched weather sirens.

Denied her own throatless howl.
Long sleeves covered bruises.
Flesh concealer applied with
an oh-so light touch disguised
black eyes; spackled white plaster
on walls hid ugly jagged fist holes.

His pinstripes fluttered as he tied perfect
Double-Winsor, ebony shoes matched belt.
He patted the dog's head, smiled winsome
smile. She watched long enough, then waved
her imaginary white-gloved hand,
the well-practiced Miss America wave.

Dog Language

I picked the house with the pretty kitchen,
glass star doorknobs, faux marbled fireplace
over what Momma called "good common sense."
Under shabby shingles, magnetic bones heard
quivered sonar impulse. Pale gray pigeon
with iron for blood, my compass found home.

Cute young cop across street, packs guns
in squad car every day at two, slowly drives
away, he eyes littered street like a hawk.
His girl stopped coming, his lips stopped smiling.

He keeps blinds pulled tight, sticks head out
for pizza deliveries, parcels from postman.

Shopping maven lives next door.
Her old man left oil spots on the drive,
boot prints on her rug, unpaid cable bills
and a mixed-breed dog chained in her back yard.
I said, 'Linda, you can't keep your dog chained
to that pole. He tangles, can't get to water…'

I thought she listened. It's said if you blink
slowly at a dog- closed eyes impart trust.
I wish I hadn't closed my ears that day
when I vacuumed cat hair from the sofa,
yacked with daughter on the phone, didn't
hear syllables yipped out in dog language.

Sharon Edge Martin *is a poet, essayist, and fiction writer, and a fifth-generation Oklahoman. She is a regular contributor to* The Oklahoma Observer *and host of a monthly poetry reading at Tidewater Winery in Drumright. Sharon's most recent books are a poetry collection,* Not a Prodigal, *which was a finalist for the Oklahoma Book Award, and a book of Observer essays,* I've Got the Blues: Looking for Justice in a Red State.

His Eye Is on the Sparrow

That's what they always told me,
but is His eye on my sick baby today?
On me?
On my husband
whose warehouse has moved
to another state?

They don't relocate minimum wage workers,
but jobs are easy to find here,
if you don't need a living wage.

Minimum wage, the minimum
they can get away with paying.

Husband has a new job.
but the same old car.
He works every day,
for a little bit of nothing
after he fills the tank.

Boss says if I can't make it to work,
I'd better look for another job.
No sick days when they cap you at 30 hours.
Can't afford to take baby to the doctor.
Can't afford daycare.
Can't afford rent, either, on one paycheck.

I wish we were sparrows. I wish someone,
anyone, was watching over
this family of mine.

God Bless These Disunited States

Thank God I live in a country
where access to health insurance
depends on where you work.

Thank God I live in a country
where state legislators with good insurance
choose not to expand Medicaid,

and public schools are funded
by ad valorem taxes, so poor kids
seldom get what they deserve,

the kind of education that breaks
the cycle of poverty
and poor health.

Bless the Constitution of my country
that still gives me the right
to speak up, to call out legislators
who don't do their job,
who expect God
to take care of their constituents for them.

Shaun Perkins *is a poet and the founder/ director of the Rural Oklahoma Museum of Poetry, a teaching artist with the Oklahoma Arts Council, a storyteller, and the co-host of two podcasts:* Wacky Poem Life *and* Okie Noir.

Montie Jean's Drugstore Calendar

This is where poetry lives:

Doris brought my iron back.
David Pierce started mowing my field.
Bertie came after her cape.
Sleet in Phoenix.
Salty ate sandwiches with us.
Quit smoking, one year.
Made 5 Easter rabbits out of bleach bottles.
First mess of polk greens.
Betty and girls stopped about 10 minutes.
Doris came out. She seemed lost without Jack.
Betty and Amos drove her school bus out to see me.
First mess of corn.
Got home about 4 p.m., a tired turd.
Catherine killing chickens.

Wash

She used to hate laundry days, the rusty
smell of boiled water poured in rough tin pans,
the cheap soap peeling away her red skin,
and the clothes coming out only half-clean.

The washing machine she cranked by hand worked
miraculously on the brown diapers
and drool on her dresses yet not so well
on the crusty sweat rings on William's shirts.

111

And now the electric multi-cycled
washer with gyrating agitator
pounds her clean sheets and blouses to an even
cleaner circle of bleached, holy softness.

She pulls up the white lid and looks inside,
smiling, wondering how she has survived.

Closet

The closet is musty with cold mildew.
Her careless sons glued the sheets of plywood
right to the concrete block foundation with
no thought of insulation or creatures.

Glue hardens quickly in the forceful wind
and then the gaps appear, the moisture drips
in, the carpet breeds green blobs, her dresses
fill with the thick damp odor of acorns.

The mice leave their black dots speckling the green.
White crickets find shelter under her shoes.
Streaks of black fungus shoot up the brown wall,
a picket fence of spongy residue.

No one but Montie knows. No one shares
the secret biology of her closet.

Shayna Mahan *I am what my husband calls "a yout" (as in, a youth, ha ha ha). An accurate description of my personality can be summed up in that I have simultaneously lived 100 lives in my 33 years and yet only lived the one that's not quite 3 years old. I have many theories on this, so should you care to hear one, find me and let me know. Anyway, I have slowly been learning more and more about poetry. I have found that most of what I have to share with the world is not as easy to read as many other poets' works, but I have also found that my poems are still welcomed by old timers and newbies alike. I am one of those that feels too much and too deeply, good and bad, joyful and painful...and poetry is becoming a beautiful way for me to learn about myself. Hopefully, someone out there will be touched in some small way by my words and think upon them when they feel too much or too deeply.*

For The Babies

For the babies...who are conceived by parents under the influence of the disease of addiction.

For the babies...who are brought into this White Man's world–where their voices will be silenced.

For the babies...who are born to parents that aren't equipped to care for them, nor do they wish to be.

For the babies...who are abandoned.
For the babies...who grow up KNOWING they are unloved and unwanted–just in the way.

For the babies...that aren't allowed to even go to school after sixth grade because they have the nerve to be born female.

For the babies...that are taught to wield weapons instead of love.

For the babies...that are taught to look up to the Donald Trump's and the Jeff Bezos' of this world–instead of Marie Curie or Amelia Earhart.

For the babies...that are stolen from family and left in cages.

For the babies...that can't be adopted because "That Couple" has the audacity to be homosexual.

For the babies...that can't feed themselves or have access to clean fucking water.

For the babies...that are born withdrawing from illicit drugs and abused alcohol and daily prescribed pharmaceuticals.

For the babies...that suffer disease, malnourishment, genetic mutations that hinder their ability to live life instead of just survive it.

For the babies...that get left at the Fire Station or the QuickTrip or the local Library—the one that should be closed because those same children might stumble upon a Transgender person reading a book to them.

For the babies...that stay home alone because their single mothers can't work any more than three jobs and are still unable to afford child care, but "make too much money" to benefit from government assistance.

For the babies...that cry–alone, scared, and heartbroken.

For the babies...that aren't allowed to learn to read or write.

For the babies...that get left in hot cars or locked in closets or beaten *by the same hands that brought them into this world.*

For the babies...conceived in circumstances so degrading to the mother that it's unacceptable to talk about it.

For the babies...whose mothers can't even look at them without reliving those attacks over and over and over again.

For the babies...who don't realize that life doesn't have to be so damn hard.

For the babies...that have no one.

For the babies...that have no voice.
For the babies...that DIDN'T FUCKING ASK TO BE HERE.

For the babies...that act out in school, run around like crazy people, and refuse to learn how to make good choices because they have no other way to communicate.

For the babies.

I hope some of you out there are hurt by my words.

I hope there are those out there that I offend with these statements.

I hope and pray that I incite rage in your hearts.

I want every single person out there that says it's easier to delude themselves with the lies that have put us in this position to take just a second...*just one*...and think about someone other than themselves.

If that's me, and you're angry that I'm calling you out, good. At least you're using your own brain for a fleeting moment.

Stephanie Theban *works as a lawyer in Tulsa, Oklahoma. She is the author of a picture book,* Alfred, *illustrated by David Barrow, and published by Doodle and Peck Publishing. She writes poetry and novels. Her writing focuses on family relationships and the struggle of becoming one's own person. She is the proud mother of two young women who have managed to become wonderful persons.*

To Play Like Stevie Ray
For Chris

You were brave and you were true
And lived the life that suited you
I should have listened when I heard you say
I just want to play like Stevie Ray

Our mama was always hardest on you
Because you didn't do what she wanted you to
Make good grades and keep your head down
That was the way to avoid that frown
But you rode a motorcycle and played in a band
And smoked and drank and made a stand
And later quit college and pursued a trade
Mama never saw the good life you made.

You married a good woman and raised two good kids
And were a wonderful papa to your grandkids.
You never wanted to be the boss
But when Parkinson's caused the loss
Of the nimble movements required
To place and twist and mold the wire
You proved you could supervise.
Then you almost made good in Mama's eyes.

She never understood the lack of ambition
Or your rejection of the family tradition
To measure our value and not our worth
To prove we deserved to live from our birth

117

Until the moment of our death
To be useful and to do with every breath
She never recognized that you gave her the truth
While I never grew from the lies of my youth.

The Parkinson's stole your agility
But never took your ability
To be kind and honest and sincere
Your conscience could always be clear.
You only ever really lied
To hide the cancer growing inside
She beat you to the grave without a clue
That those damn smokes finally got you.

You had more than your share of pain
And hardship and grief and Mama's disdain.
But even through all that strife
You lived your own chosen life.
You loved and laughed and told many a story
And if there were ever an inventory
Maybe even Mama would have understood
You weren't Stevie Ray but you were pretty damn good.

You were brave and you were true
And lived the life that suited you
I should have listened when I heard you say
I just want to play like Stevie Ray.

Cuervo

The road from Albuquerque to Amarillo is long and
straight
Too much coffee and diet pop
Meant these two old people had to stop
We wished so much that we could wait.

The gas station sign was a welcome sight
We pulled off the highway at Cuervo
Grateful we'd found a place to go
But that danged building was locked up tight.

We thought we'd check the other side
I was even willing to knock on a door
But all the porches had fallen through the floor
By now we'd lost all sense of pride.

He aimed at the dark space under the stoop
While I squatted behind the Rose of Sharon
I was long past the point of carin'
If there was anyone there to snoop.

I know that it must seem very rude
To pee in someone's front garden
But we did shout beg your pardon
To say we were sorry to intrude
And it wasn't us that killed that town
It had already failed
The residents had long since bailed
It was I-40 that mowed it down.

I'm sorry I pissed on your dreams
But they were already dead.

The Home of My Mother's Fear

Two tiny houses cobbled together
Formed my mother's childhood home.

The front room abounded with furniture
The bed where grandma slept
A lumpy sofa and a couple of chairs
The piano and the secretary

119

With the old books I read again
Each time we visited
A round dining table,
Big enough to feed family and friends
And neighbors and hands
who came to help with harvest
Back when there was a harvest.

All that living crammed into one room
A bare lightbulb hanging from the ceiling
A fireplace for heat in winter
And in summer, open doors and windows
to bring the hope of a breeze
and the reality of bugs and dust.

One room stuffed with a double bed
And a twin, jammed up against the vanity
That Grandpa got by papering a neighbor's walls
A desk, with a picture of a cowboy above it
and an ashtray on it,
so Mom could hide there to smoke.

The back room had once been the dining room
A buffet and an ancient refrigerator filled one wall
Grandpa's sick bed sprawled cattycornered
in the middle of the room
So he could watch the squirrels and birds in one direction
And Saturday night wrasslin' in the other
Sometimes he sat in his chair by the fire
Rolling his own from Prince Albert in the can
Dribbling bits of tobacco and ash
Through his yellow stained fingers.

The kitchen and bathroom were once a porch
Until Grandpa coaxed running water into the house
from the well that stood on top of the hill
He wanted to do better for his family

Until one day he went to bed and stayed.
For sixteen years.

Dad hated that claw foot tub
So he rigged a shower
Behind the smokehouse
Meat must have hung there
Once upon a time
But now it was just packed with debris
Including a large wooden propeller
Racked against the ceiling
Like it wanted to fly off into the sky
And a picture with the subject trapped
Glaring out through the dirt dauber nests
built under the glass.

It's easy to be angry
My mother focused so on appearances
And respectability and stability
Then I think about how much she wanted to escape that
place
How ashamed she was of the poverty and the grime
And how she still trekked back regularly to visit her
mother
And honor the shell of a man who had been her father.

Then I understand
That she lived in fear
That those she loved would slide back
Down from affluent suburbia
To rural destitution.

It must have been painful
To live with that terror every day.

Sue Storts *is a retired psychiatrist who grew up in Oklahoma. Storts lives in Tulsa, where she spends time writing poems, short stories, and books for young people.*

She Ain't Got the Fight Left in Her

Should rush right home, get dinner on the fire,
but it's fast-food burgers cause her feet are tired.
Knows home-cooking keeps her waistline thinner.
She ain't got the fire left in her.

Paycheck's worth less than the paper it's written on.
If she tells her boss what day she's quittin' on,
she's out on the street and it'll soon be winter.
She ain't got the fight left in her.

Serving other people food, she gets an inkling,
some organizers start her to thinking.
Her only way out is Lottery Winner.
She ain't got the fight left in her.

He makes more money, though he's a beginner.
She's worked here a decade. She's the breadwinner.
Pay inequity's par for her gender.
She ain't got the fight left in her.

No health insurance. Goes to work with the flu.
Husband's sick. Kids have got it, too.
No doctor's office that they can enter.
She ain't got the fight left in her.

Poor childcare is the price she has to pay,
as a poor working woman in the USA.
Votes to help her kids but can't pick a winner.

She ain't got the fight left in her.

Working Man's Museum

My son walked into a place downtown
to learn about Woody and look around.
They wanted $12.00 and that seemed wrong,
to see his face and hear his songs.
Well, it's only $10.00 if you happen to be old.
And free if you're a kid, so he was told.
If Woody were here, he'd make it all free.
He'd never demand an admission fee.
Pay what you want or pay if you can.
Woody understood the working man.
Guy behind the counter remained undaunted.
That's not what Woody would have wanted.
Can't see the museum if you don't have the dough?
That's not the right spirit and it made him feel low.
A museum should be for the rich and the poor.
So, he said no thank you and walked out the door.

Hank's Dream

Hank worked with his hands.
He used to use tools.
When they hired a robot,
he felt like a fool.

He pushed a small button
and felt like a jerk,
while that stupid machine
did all of his work.

They gave him a title

instead of a raise.
So overtime's out,
but he stayed late most days.

He watched that contraption
whir, clank, buzz, and spin.
Hit the button and
watched it again…and again…

Till he got real grumpy
and plumb irritated,
daydreamed and thought
about stuff that he hated.

Ran home at lunchtime,
and took out his gun.
His friends all had several,
but he just had one.

Went back to the factory,
covered his ears,
and shot that damned robot
right in its gears.

It thudded and slumped,
computer chips fried.
It turned around once,
then hissed and died.

When their hearing returned,
all his co-workers cheered.
His boss even offered
to buy him a beer.

"There's nothin' to see."
Hank heard the boss say,
"Between you and me,
we all felt the same way."

Timothy Bradford *is the author of the poetry collection* Nomads with Samsonite *and the introduction to* Sadhus, *a photography book on the ascetics of South Asia. Currently, he is a Lecturer in the Expository Writing Program at the University of Oklahoma, where he co-directs the Mark Allen Everett Poetry Series and volunteers with the Writer's Guild at Joseph Harp Correctional Center.*

Doing the Right Thing

-for all the past, present, and future
members of the Writers Guild, who
do the important work of being people's
historians and abolitionists

I feel more and more like I'm an accessory to a crime.
My state cares not how people change as they do time.

We all make mistakes, big and small, short and tall.
Some get caught, some not, as we move through time.

Lack of guidance, opportunity, money makes some risk
it all. State support? Naw, the Okie standard would rather
two time.

See, this hand is love, which most round these parts
profess they believe as they play church peek-a-boo time.

But this hand is hate and too many voters can't wait
to use it straight away when it's social issue time.
Hate hands vote hard against public education, health,
justice, equity, and peace as they misconstrue time.

These hands think they're fixed in their righteous
security and piety even though no one can glue time.

And in the big river, all changes. First will become last,
last first. Holy, wicked, wicked, holy in due time.

In other words, hate hands giving hate might find
they're nabbed and labeled thugs come coup time.

And the people now locked up who found true faith
and themselves are the ones who will outdo time.

I've always felt everyone deserves human dignity but
the Writers Guild taught Timothy its depths and true
time.

Answers for the Proletariat

Point of view narrator first-person narrator first-person
observer unreliable third-person narrator omniscient
editorializing central consciousness stream of
consciousness character protagonist dynamic
antagonist sympathetic plot flashback equilibrium
conflict epiphany exposition rising action climax falling
action resolution setting atmosphere or mood
projection enveloping action symbol universal
symbols conventional symbols literary symbols
analogy motif theme overlooking the River Niger see
wealth his grandmother's powwow-dance regalia
sympathetic New York City heroin uncle/brother pain
and suffering picture tattoo language robot hypertext
werewolves piss she is an overachiever lick she does
not truly feel at home fox heroic tales in which she
rescues somebody climax he is dismissive third-
person omniscient Vietnam various it was like
watching a rock fall Oklahoma City various various
the desert Southwest mythology shoots the rancher
musical lyric speaker audience rhetorical paraphrase
syntax figurative tone irony image metaphor simile
symbolic action prosody rhyme stanzas enjambment
feet prayer sonnet honeymoon sea singing

indifference love his mother let go personification the tiger Philippines love/desire sister garage all these things pregnancy suicide pentameter.

Tom Murphy *recently retired, was the 2021-2022 Corpus Christi Poet Laureate and the Langdon Review's 2022 Writer-In-Residence. Murphy's books are:* When I Wear Bob Kaufman's Eyes *(2022),* Snake Woman Moon *(2021),* Pearl *(2020),* American History *(2017), and he co-edited* Stone Renga *(2017). He's been published widely in literary journals and anthologies such as:* Poetry is DEAD: An Inclusive Anthology of Deadhead Poetry, Boundless, Concho River Review, MONO, Good Cop/Bad Cop Anthology, Odes and Elegies: Eco-Poetry from the Texas Gulf Coast, The Great American Wise Ass Poetry Anthology, Outrage: A Protest Anthology for Injustice in a Post 9/11 World *among other publications.*

Hell of a Hand

From the bottom of the deck
The workin' man's gloveless hand was delt.
Stakes too high, skimpy paycheck
Supply chain blowback, lowball cards flipped on the felt.

The boss wrestles me for each and every dollar
Shives my hours and confiscates my tools.
Words of the rich whip up my ire on Parlor
Grinds me into the pavers just to rule.

It's hard to concentrate on my workin' trade
Being told them's our enemies who stole our crumb.
Too much information, and pompous cavalcade
They want us to fight them or become a homeless bum.

Loyalty oaths, nondisclosures signatures only
A rich person would devise.
A thinking worker stands apart and lonely
Sifting their words to catch their lies.

Not looking for a handout but seeking relief.
Circus clowns and barkers' pseudo absolution.

The devil by any other clothes exacerbates grief.
Civil insurrection sweetie, "I am your retribution."

Between hammer and anvil lays the worker's card
Business is a Ponzi scheme yoking the worker's neck
Promises of prime cuts are delt as chunks of lard
The worker's worked to death to be discarded dreck.

Travis Lovin *is a father and a wanderer. He writes about the characters all around him and the places that have raised him. He's published a thing or two and he pretended to be a poet here last year.*

On Rolling a Cigarette

Use a strong paper.
Hemp or rice papers tear easily.
Use the one that feels like it was yanked from the old
testament.
You'll remember falling asleep while reading in the
rocking
chair with your daughter,
you'll remember loading trucks in Kansas City cold,
you'll remember the book of Job.

Use shag cut tobacco and use the good stuff.
It'll roll up nicely.
It'll taste like winter nights on the farm,
the smell of another log on the fire and the feel of your
sleeping
bag
on the floor of the house your great grandfather built.
The good stuff will cost and the house couldn't be
insured,
but it's worth it.

Lay the paper flat on the table in front of you.
Pour yourself a whiskey.
The gummed side is away.
You'll see it reflect whatever light is around you.
If you're lucky, maybe some dark too.
You'll tell the doctor only 2-3 drinks a week.
Grab a pinch of tobacco and spread it across the surface
of the paper.
Push the tobacco towards the center,

131

away from the edges.
I'll leave it to you to figure out what constitutes a pinch
and what it means to be centered.

Pick up your paper, carefully,
hot dog style and not hamburger style.
You'll remember r&b group salt n' peppa's "let's talk
about"
in the headphones and asking Jeffrey what sex is in the
hall before class.
You'll remember his dad worked the railroad.
You'll remember he brought a switchblade to class.
You'll remember 1991.
Take a drink of whiskey.
Use pointer fingers and thumbs,
roll up and back to form, to shape,
to forget about the holes in your boots.

Roll gently, but with some force.
Roll until it's firm, but also loose.
Roll until you feel the balance.
Roll until mom's not gone
and you can see Papaw's silhouette again
on horseback against the setting Louisiana sun.

Roll it down one last time before
you roll up and tuck the un-gummed side of the paper
against its opposite,
sliding a thumb across the length,
Lick the gum so it's ready to stick.
Lick it once, one side to the other.
Don't dally.
Keep it simple.
Drink your coffee black,
the way you were taught.
Roll up the rest of the way, all of the way,

all of the space you imagine is on the other side of the
river,
but will never see.

Choose a side to place to your lips.
Pinch off excess tobacco.
Pinch it flat.
It'll hang from the corner of your mouth in a way that
you'll forget about.
It'll hang there and get lost in your aching back,
the teeth you can't afford to fix,
the bills you can't pay
and when you remember it's there
you'll smile and it'll perk
and present itself to the flame
and you'll think about the passage from that one book
that talked about smoking to be close to god.
Something about capturing the power of the sun.
Something about pacifying hell.
You loved the words and you yanked them from the
spine
in the basement stacks of the college library and
It all still don't make sense.

Yvonne Carpenter's *life on a western Oklahoma farm shapes her work. Her latest publication is in* Oklahoma Today.

She Drives a Truck

Nine red enameled nails fan before her face,
a plane of uncreamed, mottled skin.
"Peeled right off," she frowned
at the single naked nail. "I get a mani-pedi
and wax every two weeks but I didn't drive
but five loads last pay period,
so patch this up. Going to
have a big check next week
I drove to Shreveport seven times
since I saw you last. From the time
I leave home until I'm back again, my
truck never shuts down,
idles while I catch a nap. It burns
one gallon per hour. Shutting off is hard
on the motor. I rest better in the sleeper
than in my bed at home. My truck logged
300,000 miles in five years.
The fellows tease me;
I would wonder why if they didn't.
But any one of them would be
there in a sec to walk me out of any
place I felt uneasy, My road brothers,
I call them. When I started driving most of the
action was local and west. Everything is
shifting east. We took 30 loads of gravel
to frac a well, gravel from here.
We lined up and waited, to be ready
when needed. Drive and wait.
My last trip I drove Shreveport
back to Gainesville without sleeping.
I had to pull in a rest stop there.

Place was full. I had to park on the access road.
A nap and I drove on home."
Her roper boots bore scuffs
from sitting in the driver's seat
and her jeans were butt-sprung
for the same reason but sequins
looped the back pocket.
A plain elastic held her ponytail;
she spoke meth speed;
and her pretty toes
inside those work boots
gleamed New York Red,

On the Road

His hair is still trooper short
but he now wears western plaid
rather than uniform brown.

"I have a story for every mile
of this stretch of I-40. I watched
a guy jump off this bridge, laid
down his gun like he was ready to
be calm, then paused like he just
thought "I am done," and jumped
right off the bridge. I was worried
about a cross fire between us on one side
and the police department on the other.
He jumped into the traffic below.
A truck hit him."

"I pulled a speeder over at this mile marker.
Another car, traveling with him, pulled off
ahead. That second car had no more than stopped
when a third crashed into him from behind.
That third car exploded and the driver jumped out

on fire. Was a guy carrying chemicals for
a nail shop and they exploded on impact.
No warning, instantly on fire, both car and driver.
He came running and I didn't know what to do.
Could I put him out? Would I catch fire too?
Bad, bad deal."

"I was sitting right here
when one of the worst deals started.
Two inmates escaped from Granite,
kidnapped woman and her child in Elk.
An oilfield trucker spotted the stolen van
on a county road and alerted us. I headed
north and got behind a sheriff's unit
chasing them. Became a big circus.
Guys for state and two counties plus DOC.
One of those guys held the baby out the window,
held him by the neck, wanting us to back off.
A DOC officer shot the car, killed it. Those
guys came out with their hands up. The woman
was shot in the chase.

"I was wounded along here. Had a car stopped.
Walked up, putting hands on her trunk in case
something went wrong and evidence might be needed.
Standard way to conduct a stop. Something hit me
in the back of the head. Had I been shot?
I was bleeding and my hat knocked off.
Figured later a wheel weight had fallen
off and was laying in the road.
A car spun it up and it hit me.
It would have killed me if it flew
straight off a truck."

"Yeah, I have a memory for every mile of this road."

Therapy

Her blue scrubs matched her eyes.
Three gold studs shone in her ears.

"Home health changed my theory of healing.
In the hospital, I saw my patient daily
for an hour and a half. I thought I was making them well.
Now I see my patients weekly in their homes
And they get well faster. Having more control
Being more comfortable, they heal quicker.

"The house may not be as clean
And the food less healthy,
Five little dogs may nip at their feet;
mice might feed on the counters;
drafts come around the windows;
grandson may leave a drug pipe on the coffee table,
but they get better faster.

"GPS has helped
but I like oral directions for the rural visits.
Which roads flood and when are deer active?
I drive 200 miles some days,

"I find some way to relate, to get them to talk.
Telling their stories, such interesting lives,
finding ways to organize their words when
the brain doesn't work the way it used to.

"One goal is to organize a task,
like making a ham sandwich.
Well, if this man has never made a sandwich,
he might have changed the oil in his truck.
I help him find words to recall and put
that memory into words.

"Everybody's mind works differently.
One woman can visualize the word,
spell it, then say that word she could not find.
Another can talk about the function of a thing,
go all around it, finally nail the illusive word.
"I hear about the horses he trained,
the cotton she picked, ration books they hoarded,
children loved and family lost.
My job is to help them find a way to function
when the brain has changed and old methods don't work.

"I love my work."

Zhenya Yevtushenko *currently resides in Tulsa, Oklahoma where he is finishing his undergraduate education hoping to become a teacher and literary translator. His work and translations have been published in* The Guardian, eMerge Magazine, Right Hand Pointing, The Tulsa Review, *and* Suburban Witchcraft Magazine, *among other journals. He owes his inspiration to his mother, his brothers, and to the love of his life, Olivia.*

Invisible

I don't know the rules of your game anymore
the way a callous unlearns the hand
invisible, am I still essential?
A hero slings sandwiches like masterpieces.
The way a callous unlearns the hand
an old song doesn't die with the singer,
a hero slinging sandwiches like masterpieces
as supply will predecease demand.
An old song doesn't die with the singer
invisible, am I still essential?
As supply will predecease demand

I don't know the rules of your game anymore.

Are You Ready to Order?

This is okay for now, clearly you have a lot of promise,
this is temporary, right?

Oh hold on, more creamer, more jelly, more coffee, more
napkins, more hot sauce.

You wanna know a secret to save money? Don't tip on
the sales tax.

You should write that down.

The following authors have provided previous publications information for their poems:

Alan Berecka:
"Blue Collar Heaven," "The Builder of Bigger Angel Dance Floors," and "Vocational Education" *A Living is Not a Life: A Working Title* (Black Spruce Press, 2021) "The Builder of Bigger Angel Dance Floors," first appeared in *Concho River Review;* "Vocational Education" first appeared in *Windward Review*

Julie Chappell:
"Holiday Joys" *Faultlines: One Woman's Shifting Boundaries.* (Village Books Press, 2013).
"At the QT" *Mad Habits of a Life.* (Lamar University Literary Press, 2019).
"Badges for My Father" *As I Pirouette Away.* (Turning Plow Press, 2021).

Hank Jones:
"Digging a Grave," "My Season in Hell," and "Too Late for Manly Hands" *Too Late for Manly Hands* (Turning Plow Press, 2021).

Ken Hada:
"We Have These Witnesses" *Way of the Wind* (Fine Dog Press, 2019)
"Janitor" *Bring an Extry Mule,* (VACpoetry, 2017)
"The Working Poor" *Not Quite Pilgrims* (VACpoetry, 2019)